WITHD
WRIGHT STATE UN. Y0-CAJ-037

COLS WRIGHT STATE UNIVERSITY
UNIVERSITY LIBRARY

0 0013 0158830 5

DATE DUE

AUG 0 8 1994			

HIGHSMITH 45-220

EXCELLENCE and EQUALITY

SUNY Series
FRONTIERS IN EDUCATION
Philip G. Altbach, Editor

The Frontiers in Education Series features and draws
upon a range of disciplines and approaches in the
analysis of educational issues and concerns, helping to
reinterpret established fields of scholarship in education
by encouraging the latest synthesis and research.

Other books in this series include:

Class, Race, and Gender in American Education
— Lois Weis (ed.)

EXCELLENCE and EQUALITY

A QUALITATIVELY DIFFERENT PERSPECTIVE
ON GIFTED AND TALENTED EDUCATION

DAVID M. FETTERMAN

State University of New York Press

LC
3993.9
.F48
1988

Published by
State University of New York Press, Albany

©1988 State University of New York

All rights reserved

Printed in the United States of America

No part of this book may be used or reproduced
in any manner whatsoever without written permission
except in the case of brief quotations embodied in
critical articles and reviews.

For information, address State University of New York
Press, State University Plaza, Albany, N.Y., 12246

Library of Congress Cataloging-in-Publication Data

Fetterman, David M.
  Excellence and equality.

  (SUNY series, frontiers in education)
  Includes index.
  1. Gifted children — Education — United States.
  2. Gifted children — Education — Cross-cultural studies.
  3. Educational equalization — United States.
  4. Educational equalization — Cross-cultural studies.
  I. Title. II. Series.
  LC3993.9.F48 1988   371.95   87-10078
  ISBN 0-88706-640-2
  ISBN 0-88706-641-0 (pbk.)

10 9 8 7 6 5 4 3 2 1

This book is dedicated to my younger brother

Roy Ivan Fetterman

July 17, 1958 – September 11, 1986
whose gift was an unbounded spirit.

Contents

Foreword

Dr. Fetterman presents an intelligent, far-ranging approach to excellence and equality. He covers much ground in this unique treatment of issues in the identification and facilitation of talented youths, especially those who excel intellectually. As an anthropologist and educationalist, he considers them at local, state, national, and international levels. Especially valuable is his detailed discussion of "elitism," democracy "versus" excellence, and self-fulfillment "versus" the technological future of the United States.

Dr. Fetterman's work highlights many of the problems facing the education of gifted and talented persons. In his opinion, "most serious obstacles include hostility and complacency toward the gifted, resulting in educational neglect." To him, "educational neglect is a silent time bomb threatening the quality of life for us all."

Examination of over 433 programs in the State of California by Dr. Fetterman illustrates the diversity of programs available for gifted and/or talented children. His case study of a program in the midwestern United States represents a national test case for gifted-child education and minority enrollment. The book benefits greatly from these two empirical studies that he carried out.

This volume seems to me a distinctive contribution to the professional literature about gifted children. It speaks forcefully to educators, gifted youths and their parents, and policy makers at various levels, including those in colleges and universities.

I shall now make a few personal observations, to which Dr. Fetterman also subscribes. One cannot stress enough the extreme importance of early identification of intellectually talented boys and girls and the *academic* facilitation of those from the point of identification all the way through their education to the highest degree attained. Rather than "teachers of the gifted," which is almost a contradiction in terms, or at least as supplements to their efforts, we need coordinators of special, academically oriented educational opportunities for the gifted. These coordinators find and/or devise in-school and out-of-school educational experiences that supplement or replace some age-in-grade classes. They strive for curricular flexibility and proper articulation of learning in school with academic competencies acquired formally or informally elsewhere. They bring to bear a vast array of possibilities, depending on many ability, geographical, and sociological considerations, to devise for each gifted student each year an appropriate overall curriculum. They seek for these students opportunities to enter academic competitions within the school, locality, state, nation, and world. Thus, the gifted individuals can hone their intellects against their true intellectual peers. In doing so they can interact with their mental equals or superiors socially while acquiring some of the rigorous intellectual "lore" needed to succeed at progressively more demanding work.

This should also help counteract the anguish of being considered merely a "brain" in the local classroom. Where high intellectual level is the common denominator of a group, its members are freer to act as human beings rather than as stereotyped cerebral cortexes entrapped in a corner of the classroom with their intellectual fangs bared. High-level academic summer programs seem especially helpful in bringing out the best in intellectually talented youths, reducing their sense of isolation, and lessening whatever arrogance they may have had at the start of the program. Academic demands consonant with intellectual abilities often produce startlingly excellent learning and improved socialization.

More use needs to be made of diagnostic testing followed by precisely prescribed instruction so that much of the intellectually talented boy's or girl's time in the classroom will not be wasted. What does the student not yet know, and how can he or she learn it well at a pace suited to the individual's actual mental ability? For this, individualized tutoring or "mentoring" of groups of from one to about five students is often best.

There are many ways to identify gifted youths and nurture them academically. Dr. Fetterman considers a number of them, so I shall stop this brief introduction in order that the eager reader may savor the book itself.

Julian C. Stanley
Professor of Psychology and
Director of the Study of Mathematically
Precocious Youth at Johns Hopkins University

Preface

The first part of the title of this book, *Excellence and Equality,* crystallizes a basic tension in American society: How do we foster excellence and yet maintain equality? What are the trade-offs when we stress one goal over the other? This book is built on the assumption that both goals are good and necessary if we are to maintain our commitment to quality, our democratic ideals, and our multi-cultural traditions. The strength and vitality of our nation and all nations are dependent on the gifts and talents of individuals. A highly educated citizenry can make informed and knowledgeable decisions to maintain and improve the quality of their lives, individually and as a whole.

At the same time it is important to recognize the constraining forces of culture. In American culture and in the cultures of other egalitarian nations, the balance between individual and even group excellence and equality is at best difficult to achieve. The tension is not as great in physical or psychomotor achievements as it is in the intellectual sphere. Athletic achievement, excellence, and superiority are recognized in American culture. However, few of us like to think about intellectual superiority — unless we are in the emergency room in need of the brightest physician available. Often an equality of rights and opportunities is confused with an equality of ability and achievement. A classic tension is created when individuals or cooperative groups are encouraged to fulfill their potential and strive for excellence in the midst of a cultural ethos that reminds each of us not to stand out too far from the group. But gifted children by definition stand out from the group. The existence of gifted and talented education programs begs the question: Special privilege or special need? This book confronts that tension — in American culture and throughout the world — by explicitly focusing on how gifted and talented education programs balance educational excellence with equal educational opportunity, ability, and achievement.

The second part of the title, *A Qualitatively Different Perspective on Gifted and Talented Education,* is a play on the definition of gifted and talented education — which provides a ''qualitatively different educational experience'' to meet the needs of these children. This book is qualitatively different from other texts in the field in many respects.

First, whereas there is much written about what does not work in gifted and talented education, this book focuses on what does work in these programs. In the process of describing and evaluating how gifted and talented education programs are working throughout the world, a model of educational excellence is derived and discussed in terms of its generalizability to the mainstream educational system.

Second, most textbooks in gifted and talented education are written from a psychological perspective. This is a valuable approach, but there are other lenses through which to view the field. The research presented in this book was conducted by an anthropologist. The studies discussed in this text intentionally introduce an anthropological point of view for nonanthropological scholars, educators, evaluators, legislators, and the general public — as well as for other anthropologists. Anthropological techniques and concepts are employed to address basic social problems in education and to influence a concerned public outside the field of anthropology. Anthropological methods are generally descriptive in nature and are useful in providing a picture of what is really going on in classrooms, schools, and districts. These methods are typically used to gain the ''insiders' '' perspective on their role in the educational system. Information comes not primarily from tests, but from lengthy interviews with students, teachers, parents, administrators, and other individuals — both supporters and detractors of gifted and talented education. Intensive, long-term participation (over three years in one of the studies reported) in the school programs and in the students', teachers', and coordinators' homes, as well as observation of program participants and other individuals in these programs and after school, were essential information-gathering techniques. Daily observation of classroom behavior anchored the research effort in the daily lives of gifted children and educators. Informal and formal interviews with students, parents, and teachers in their homes or in other casual settings provided honest insights into their view of reality. Discussions held in nonthreatening environments alleviated many of the problems that can be associated with interviews restricted to the school environment, where everyone wears a slightly different mask and assumes a somewhat more formal posture. I provided an anthropological, descriptive account and made a conceptual leap to assess or evaluate what I found. (See Fetterman 1984a, Fetterman and Pitman 1986, and Fetterman 1988 for information about the emerging role of anthropology and evaluation.) The findings discussed in this book were derived from a multicultural and evaluative perspective — from viewing the problem on local, state, national, and international levels.

Finally, this text makes specific educational policy recommendations. The most significant recommendation involves the reauthorization of a national center for the gifted to revitalize gifted and talented education and in the process to serve as a beacon of educational excellence for the entire educational system. In addition, a recommendation is made to establish a national school for the gifted, much like West Point in New York State, for the development of the best young gifted and talented minds. As noted earlier, a model of educational excellence derived from studies of successful gifted and talented educational programs across the globe is presented with the aim of generalizing critical elements to the mainstream educational system. Key elements worthy of adoption include quality, commitment, leadership, diversity of curriculum and instruction, and a whole-person approach to education. A useful model developed at Stanford University for university-level gifted and talented education conferences is also presented. This type of conference brings gifted students, parents, teachers, administrators, and colleagues together. Gifted students are provided an opportunity to establish a link with exemplary researchers. Academic career decisions can be discussed with input from a variety of valuable sources in one setting. The multilevel conference can be a valuable offering at colleges and universities throughout the United States and abroad. Moreover, this type of conference serves to forge stronger bonds between secondary and postsecondary institutions. It is hoped that this book will provide a healthy new direction for our entire educational system and simultaneously help to meet the needs of the gifted.

D.M.F.

Acknowledgments

A study of this size, complexity, and duration could not have been completed without the assistance of literally thousands of individuals. Although thanking each individual is impossible, I would like to mention a few.

First, I am indebted to Bob, Dan, Jennifer, Eddie, Kisha, and hundreds of other gifted children and their parents throughout the country. They have generously shared their lives with me, both in the schools and in their homes. In return, I hope this book responds to their personal and academic concerns.

Second, I greatly appreciate the work and the commitment of those gifted teachers whose efforts and creativity enabled me to document a qualitatively different educational experience for gifted children. In addition to their daily practice, their insights into gifted and talented education helped shape my understanding of the current status of the field. A few of the exceptional teachers who spent time with me above and beyond the call of their duties include Bonnie Deming, Chris Dickerson, Punky Fristrom, Margo Kluth, Maria Lipton, Gary Millen, Brad Powers, Willa Ramsay, Edmund Sutro, Jan Talbot, Tim Tanzer, and Barbara Quickstad. In addition, several teachers were extraordinarily helpful to me in researching this study, including Barnes, Hinkley, Owens, Roshko, and Zweers.

Third, my thanks are extended to gifted coordinators throughout the country who have been instrumental in orchestrating gifted and talented programs. These individuals have helped me understand the strengths and weaknesses of their district programs and have facilitated the daily execution of my duties on the site. A few coordinators warrant special consideration, notably Bruce DeVries, Dave

Hermanson, Jan Horner, Mary Anne Kane, Elizabeth Kearney, and Cindy Silbert.

A politically savvy principal adds immeasurably to the strength of a gifted and talented program. Such an individual's knowledge, combined with an instinct for survival, guides programs through the turbulent waters of educational politics. I am grateful to those principals who were open about the politics of their school systems. Their willingness to share their cultural knowledge of the school system helped me conduct my research and avoid many of the pitfalls that often accompany research in education. D. George Burdette, John Garrett, George Montello, Bill Rosencranz, and Peter Schroeder provided particularly valuable political information during this study.

The commitment of board of education members, superintendents, research directors, and concerned citizens is also fundamental to the success of any program for gifted children. These individuals are responsible for steering their programs through the hazardous terrain of competing programs in the district. The time and effort these people devoted to answering my often naive questions contributed greatly to my research. Representatives who devoted additional personal time to the completion of this study include Ross Canterbury, Kay Davis, Mac Frederick, Edward Griffith, David J. Walvoord, and Harry Whitaker.

The California Association for the Gifted provided a forum for many of the findings discussed in this study — both at executive meetings and at professional association meetings. I am grateful to the former presidents of the association who helped guide me through numerous site visits to programs for the gifted and talented in California. Bob Swain, Jeanne Delp, Miriam Surface, and Jean Wienner were particularly valuable consultants during intensive site visits. They each provided a cross-check on my analysis of the programs. Former presidents Allyn Arnold and Sandy Kaplan provided insightful comments on evaluation reports about programs in California. Their comments refined the results reported in this study. In addition, Sandy's continued generosity in exchanging ideas and materials is greatly appreciated.

I am also indebted to Barbara Brandes for her intelligent and judicious monitoring of the California study. The tireless efforts of the state special projects officer and the GATE (Gifted and Talented Education) management team, including Edward Bispo, Elinor McKinney, Jack Mosier, and Paul Plowman, contributed greatly to this study. Barbara, the current GATE director, Linda Forsyth, and Jeffrey Zettel at the State Department of Education have also helped me keep abreast of state and national issues.

Consulate attachés and academic colleagues across the globe were very helpful in providing information about gifted programs in their countries. Special thanks are extended to B.I. Kozyr' from the Academy of Pedagogical Sciences and V. Bakhurov, representing the American Consulate General of the Union of Soviet Socialist Republics; Kurt Heller and Cornelia Facaoaru from Universitat Munchen; Blanka Burg of the Department for Gifted Children in Israel; Ernest House from the University of Illinois at Urbana-Champaign; George Parkyn from New Zealand; Francisca Soriano, representing the Philippine Consulate General; Julieta Savellano, dean of the College of Education at the University of the Philippines; Erlinda Camara, chairperson of the Filipino Gifted, Talented, and Creative Study at the University of the Philippines; Cleofe M. Bacungan, director of the Philippine Science High School; Conny Semiawan, representing the Ministry of Education and Culture in Jakarta; S. Munandar from Universitas Indonesia in Jakarta; Abdessalam Diab, representing the Embassy of the Arab Republic of Egypt; Rubaya Thalib, representing the Republic of Indonesia; Jakub Isman, representing the Embassy of Indonesia; Hisako Takahashi and Joyce Yukawa from the Consulate General of Japan; the attaché from Brazil; and colleagues, especially Chen Guomei, from the Department of Education at Beijing Normal University in China.

I am particularly appreciative of the efforts of F.W. Conrad, representing the Generalkonsulat der Bundesrepublik Deutschland. His assistance in securing essential primary and secondary materials to document the history of education for the gifted in West Germany proved to be of great importance. Similarly, Arthur J. Cropley from the University of Hamburg generously shared his thoughts and prepublished manuscript covering the proceedings of the Sixth World Conference on Gifted and Talented Children. I would also like to thank David Pur, head of the Pedagogical Secretariat Ministry of Education and Culture in Israel, for his company and illuminating conversation during his stay at Stanford University. His knowledge of the larger sociopolitical context of programs for the gifted enabled me to place the Israeli programs in proper perspective.

I extend my thanks also to my colleagues in the School of Education and in the Anthropology Department at Stanford

University. Edward Haertel provided useful technical advice about some of the statistical analysis of the Peoria data. Denis Phillips helped me crystallize my understanding of the Australian and New Zealand cultural context. Lee Shulman and David Tyack's insightful contribution during the final stages of the manuscript proved to be extremely useful. David Rogosa, from the School of Education, and Brad Efron, from the Statistics Department, provided much-needed material about the mathematically precocious in the United States. In addition, they helped sensitize me to the dwindling supply of mathematical talent in our country. My conversations with Milbrey McLaughlin about House's work in Illinois were instructive and appreciated. George Spindler's communications about cultural transmission and his firsthand knowledge of Mead's work with the gifted were exceptionally valuable.

Chris Wood provided project direction and survey expertise in the California study. She is also one of the most diligent and dedicated colleagues with whom I have had the pleasure to work on any evaluation. Paul Hanna and Jerry Dorfman provided support and the encouragement needed to bring this manuscript to fruition. I cannot begin to express the depth of my appreciation for their assistance. In addition, the Advisory Committee for the Hanna Collection provided invaluable comments that helped to refine this book. Members included Philip Altbach, William Brickman, R. Freeman Butts, Philip Coombs, Robert Leestma, Charles Palm, Ralph Tyler, and Donald Warren. I am also indebted to Hilja Kukk, Hoover Institution librarian, for her assistance in translating Russian texts and correspondence throughout this study. My gratitude is extended to Julian Stanley and Robert Sternberg for their helpful comments on earlier drafts of this effort.

I appreciate editorial permission to reprint my articles, in part or in whole, from several sources, including the following: D.M. Fetterman, Gifted and Talented Education in the Soviet Union, *Gifted Education International*, 1987, 4(3):180-183; and D.M. Fetterman, Gifted and Talented Education: A National Test Case in Peoria, *Educational Evaluation and Policy Analysis*, 1986a, 8(2):155 – 166.

This work is built on a foundation constructed by Lewis Terman, Robert Sears, and international contemporary luminaries in the field of gifted and talented education such as James Gallagher, Dorothy Sisk, Julian Stanley, and A. Henry Passow. This study has also been strongly influenced by such figures as Clark, Khatena, Renzulli, and Torrence, among many others in the field.

Finally, I would like to thank Rilla Klipper for her coordination efforts, Kermit Patton for the graphic art contribution, and Deborah S. Waxman for her patience with me, her support, and her insightful assistance, with Judith Clay Lhamon, in the preparation of this manuscript.

CHAPTER 1

Gifted and Talented Education: A National Priority

The time is ripe for a reevaluation of gifted and talented education programs. The huge volume of commissioned reports on education has awakened the nation to educational concerns. The Richardson study (Cox, Daniel, and Boston 1985) has specifically focused attention on able learners, a group that includes the gifted and the high achiever. Technological tragedies in the aerospace industry and the threat of foreign competition have shaken our confidence and pointed to the urgency of properly preparing tomorrow's leaders.

This study reevaluates the role of gifted and talented education worldwide and argues that this educational arena must become a national priority if we are to survive and prosper in the international marketplace. Gifted programs prepare future leaders, scientists, and artists. In addition, these programs help meet the individual needs of gifted children. The loss in unrealized potential of underserved gifted children is incalculable — in lost inventions, cures, discoveries, and dreams. Gifted programs help gifted students maximize their potential and increase the probability that they will make a productive contribution to society.

The study also explores the multifaceted nature of gifted and talented education programs to enhance the understanding and sensitivity of educators, policymakers, and the general public to the value of these programs. The study provides a unique evaluation of programs and models across the globe. Moreover, it offers an anthropological view of these programs, providing detailed descriptions of gifted and talented education programs to complement the mainstream psychological approach to this field.

Gifted and talented education must overcome many obstacles if students and programs are to fulfill their potential. This work

highlights many of the problems facing gifted and talented education. The most serious obstacles include hostility and complacency
toward the gifted, which result in neglect. Educational neglect is the
silent time bomb of our generation that will explode in the next,
threatening the quality of life for all of us.

An examination of one of the leading gifted programs in the
nation — California's Gifted and Talented Education (GATE)
program — aims to do the following:

1. Demonstrate the diversity of available programs
2. Identify significant attributes that make these programs work
3. Illustrate the effort of a large-scale program to diversify its
gifted program population
4. Reveal the larger social and political influences currently
inhibiting the development of gifted and talented programs.

An issue that emerges from this study and that lies at the heart
of the field is equal opportunity. Gifted programs rarely have proportional minority representation. California's effort to diversify its
population is one manifestation of this sociocultural dilemma. A case
study of a program in the midwestern United States represents a
national test case for gifted education and minority enrollment. A
study of this case identifies underlying socioeconomic factors that
help explain disproportionate minority enrollment figures. The
discussion then turns to an exploration of national issues with an
international perspective. A look at how gifted programs fare cross-
culturally demonstrates that the needs of the gifted are recognized
in varying degrees and fashions — even in those nations whose
ideologies emphasize egalitarianism over individuality. In addition,
this review captures a more penetrating and pervasive problem
underlying gifted and talented education: the balance between
individual and societal needs. A review of international programs
also highlights our need to shake ourselves out of a national complacency about the gifted. We need to compare our efforts with those
of other nations and then work to revitalize existing programs. We
can also borrow the most valuable strategies from gifted and talented
programs at home and abroad to restore the United States's educational system as a whole. A generalizable model of program features
drawn from this research endeavor serves as a beacon of excellence
for educational programs in the United States and throughout the
world.

Equal Educational Opportunity

Equal educational opportunity is the right of all children. Educational programs have been developed to help the disenfranchised and disabled reach their potential and meaningfully contribute to society. Gifted educational programs have been developed to meet the needs of the gifted child. Unfortunately, the development of gifted programs lags behind that of all other comparable educational programs, including vocational, handicapped, and migrant education programs.

The term *equal educational opportunity* is often associated with the socioeconomically disadvantaged, and discussions of this concept generally reach esoteric levels of abstraction. However, equal educational opportunity is a real issue in the daily lives of gifted children of all socioeconomic backgrounds in educational institutions throughout the United States. Gifted children are often denied the opportunity to develop their potential.

Bill is a typical highly gifted child. A second-grade child with an IQ of 148, Bill is intellectually several grades ahead of his chronological peers. He is restless and disruptive in class because school has no meaning for him. He is becoming more withdrawn socially as well. Bill spends less time socializing with other children of his age and more time reading and watching educational programming. At home, he has become increasingly destructive; his parents have run out of constructive activities to occupy his mind. Bill's mother asked the school principal if Bill could be admitted to a special program. The principal threw his hands up in the air and said, "Program! I don't think we've even got another kid in the school with an IQ like his, never mind a program. There is nothing we can do, except return him to his regular classroom." Bill's mother explained, "It's like my child has a handicap and there is no one out there who's willing to help." She was frustrated by an educational system that was neither able nor willing to meet her halfway. The principal was insensitive to and ignorant of the needs of gifted children. The system for identifying gifted children was haphazard. No educational or counseling program existed in the school. Alternatives such as acceleration, enrichment, or transfer to another school in the district were not offered or considered. When Bill's mother asked whether Bill could be transferred to an all-day gifted program in another school district, the principal was more concerned with district enrollment and funding than with proper placement of this child. The educational system had failed her and her child, and the individual costs of this failure were already becoming apparent. Unfortunately, this story is not unique. Gifted children are often denied equal educational opportunity to develop their potential. This problem is not only an individual problem or a local school problem; it is a national problem of enormous magnitude, a reflection of a maladaptive national attitude that is intolerant of individual differences. As Gardner (1961) points out:

> We might as well admit that it is not easy for us as believers in democracy to dwell on the differences in capacity between men. Democratic philosophy has tended to ignore such differences where possible, and to belittle them where it could not ignore them. . . . But extreme equalitarianism — or as I would prefer to say, *equalitarianism wrongly conceived* — which ignores differences in native capacity and achievement, has not served democracy well. . . . it means the end of that striving for excellence which has produced mankind's greatest achievements. (pp. 14–15)

This issue strikes at the heart of our national educational problem.

A National Problem

We are a nation at risk, according to the National Commission on Excellence in Education (1983). The Commission explained: "Our once unchallenged preeminence in commerce, industry, science, and technological innovation is being overtaken by competitors throughout the world" (p. 5). Similar fears have been expressed by the Business-Higher Education Forum in its recent report, *America's Competitive Challenge: The Need for a National Response* (1983). This report points to the "growing evidence that the United States is falling behind competitively" (p. 4). The Twentieth Century Fund Task Force in Federal Elementary and Secondary Education Policy and the National Science Board (in its report *Education in Science and Technology*) have also joined in this alarming chorus, along with more than twenty similar educational task forces. (See Passow 1984 for one of the most thorough and critical reviews of these national reports.)

Each of these commissions has identified the declining quality of American education as the underlying cause of our current dilemma. Public opinion supports this view. A 1983 Gallup Poll of public attitudes toward public schools indicated that the public believes that education is the foundation on which we build the future of our country. The National Commission on Excellence in Education reported that "the educational foundations of our society are presently being eroded by a rising tide of mediocrity that threatens our very future as a Nation and a people" (p. 5). Goodlad (1984) presents an even bleaker picture: "American schools are in trouble. In fact, the problems of schooling are of such crippling proportions that many schools may not survive. It is possible that our entire public education system is nearing collapse" (p. 242).

These reports are a long-overdue call for a return to excellence in education. Public interest in restoring the quality of education is evidenced by a recent Gallup Poll, which reported that the public believes that "education should be at the top of the Nation's agenda." There is much work to do in revitalizing the nation's educational system to prepare for the country's competitive role in the global society.

The critical question is, Where shall we begin? Teachers must adopt higher expectations of students. High school graduation requirements must be strengthened. Universities should adopt more rigorous academic standards and admission requirements. Students should be assigned more homework. Higher standards for teacher certification and increased salaries for teachers are essential. We need to instill a commitment to "lifelong learning." Clearly, our entire educational system must be improved for all individuals. A variety of areas in our educational system require attention. The Stanford and the Schools project, Harvard's Institute for Principals, Berkeley's Bay Area Writing Project, and the University of Florida's Community in the Classroom Model Program are only a few of the successful approaches currently directed at our national problem. Another approach is to use preexisting structures within the educational system more effectively. A logical place to focus our energy is the area where we can maximize our scarce resources with the highest probability of success — that is, by focusing on students with the greatest potential: gifted and talented children.

A Question of Neglect

Gifted children represent one of the greatest assets of any society and are an integral part of the intellectual spirit and vitality of the future. Ironically, gifted children are one of our most underused resources. The paucity of fiscal resources allocated to gifted programs results from a bewildering set of educational policy priorities. In 1983, the State of California expended $16.8 million on two hundred thousand students currently enrolled in gifted programs, an increase of $1.2 million over 1980–81 funding. Given inflation, this figure is actually a decrease in real money, with a corresponding increase of forty thousand gifted students. Between 1980 and 1983, the average per-pupil expenditure in gifted programs decreased from $97 to $84. This figure takes on added significance when compared to expenditures of $153 million and $63 million for competing educational programs with populations of similar size. Contrary to expectations, funding of gifted programs does not even match that of comparable programs with different but equally worthy goals. This inequity is typical of state funding patterns throughout the United States. As Gallagher (1985) reports: ''The states have varied widely in their willingness or ability to provide financial help to local school systems for program support. . . . There was about $150 million committed and a total of over nine hundred thousand students receiving some type of special service in 1981. This still left an estimated six hundred thousand plus gifted students receiving no special support from the state level'' (pp. 373–374). (See also Mitchel 1981 for details.)

Moreover, significant obstacles have been erected by shortsighted detractors of gifted education. These obstacles include lack of funding for programs, charges of elitism or an egalitarian suspicion of the gifted, and apathy. All of these obstacles result in educational neglect. Children at either margin of educational institutions suffer from a system geared toward the average student. Gifted children are often forced to follow a rigid curriculum that they have mastered long ago, resulting in terminal boredom and disillusionment with the educational system. The educational system is designed to meet the needs of the majority — not the disadvantaged minority. Schools should provide children with an education tailored to their intellectual needs — whether they have learning disabilities or extraordinary capabilities. As Stanley (1980) suggests, ''the age-in-grade, Carnegie-unit lockstep . . . for instruction in academic school subjects has crept insidiously upon us as we have moved from tutorial instruction and the one-room school house to the current situation. . . . [and it] needs to be reversed''(p. 11).

The general public recognized the value of gifted children in the early sixties. The Soviet Union's Sputnik launched this country into a technological race, the effects of which we are only beginning to understand and appreciate. This intellectual marathon engaged the talents and imagination of the nation and awakened us to the importance of a neglected resource — gifted children.

California has been a leader in developing educational programs for gifted children, primarily as a result of the political pressures exerted by a small but dedicated and vocal parent organization. The State of California established a formal program for gifted students in 1961, the Mentally Gifted Minor (MGM) program, which served those students who scored in the upper 2 percent of individually administered intelligence tests. The MGM program faced the same difficulties and charges of elitism that gifted programs nationwide confront today. The majority of intellectually gifted students in MGM programs were from communities with high socioeconomic status. The problem took on racial implications because blacks were underrepresented in these communities. In 1980, the name and structure of the MGM program changed. New legislation (AB 1040) transformed the MGM program into the GATE program. GATE legislation broadened the target population of the program. Whereas the old program had focused exclusively on intellectual abilities, the GATE program includes both the intellectually gifted and students of demonstrated high achievement. It also includes students with specific academic talents, creativity, leadership, and abilities in visual and performing arts. GATE legislation encourages experimentation with programmatic approaches, cost levels, and identification procedures of the district-level programs.

Program evaluations are considered an instrumental force in maintaining the quality of these programs and in ensuring that state and federal mandates are followed as prescribed (see Alexander and Muia 1982; Archambault 1984; Aylesworth 1984; Barnette 1984; Buescher 1984a; Callahan and Caldwell 1984; Davis and Rimm 1985; Gallagher 1985; Newland 1976; Renzulli 1975, 1984; Tannenbaum 1983; and Tuttle 1978 regarding the role of evaluation in gifted and talented programs). The California State Department of Education granted RMC Research Corporation, a Mountain View-based educational research corporation, a contract to evaluate California's GATE program. The evaluation required the use of survey and qualitative or ethnographic techniques to document the current status of the gifted programs throughout California over a three-year period (Wood and Fetterman 1981, 1983). The study focused on the impact of the legislative reforms. "The intent of the legislative reforms was that the program expand and diversify its population" (Wood 1985, p. 287). The survey portion of the study demonstrated that "the program has shown slow gradual progress in moving toward full implementation of the legislation as evidenced by the use of new categories of identification and changes in the racial/ethnic composition of the participants." Clearly, however, "without increases in present funding levels it is unlikely that full implementation can be achieved" (Wood 1985, p. 287).

The ethnographic portion of the evaluation also produced a number of significant findings on educational policy at the program, school district, and state levels (see Fetterman 1984a, and Fetterman and Pitman 1986 for the use of ethnographic evaluation). Moreover, the qualitative portion of the study responds to Stanley and Benbow's recommendation that "research should be pursued on the causes of the great hostility toward precocious intellectual achievement that is endemic in this country and on ways to counteract it" (1982, p. 8). The ethnographic component of the study revealed the larger social and political influences currently inhibiting the development of these programs. The study also addressed internal disorders that attack the program from within. On a broader level, the obstacles faced by the GATE program strike at the heart of what is wrong with our educational system. The lessons learned from this study suggest a number of constructive alternatives to our current course. In addition, useful educational models drawn from gifted programs, focusing on high standards and training in critical thinking, are generalizable to the educational mainstream.

The first step toward understanding the undervalued and frequently misunderstood role of gifted children and gifted education in the United States is to place gifted education in both ideological and historical perspective. The question of special privilege or special need is at the heart of this national dilemma. This chapter attempts to place our problem in its cultural context by presenting the larger social and political influences that shape gifted education.

Special Privilege or Special Need?

The most significant obstacle to the GATE program observed throughout the three-year study was the belief of parents, teachers, administrators, local policymakers, and state legislators that gifted children were given special privileges rather than participating in educational programs that answered their special needs. Yet significant numbers of gifted students in regular programs have become dropouts both mentally and physically — usually as a result of sheer boredom. In fact, the National Commission on Excellence in Education has emphasized that "over half the population of gifted students do not match their tested ability with comparable achievement in school" (p. 8). Such students are forced to follow lock-step programs in the regular school curriculum whose content they have mastered years ago. Instead of being challenged, gifted children are encouraged to rest on their laurels and even hide their talents and abilities. The National Commission on Excellence in Education recognized that "the most gifted students . . . need a curriculum enriched and accelerated beyond even the needs of other students of high ability" (p. 24). Gifted programs enable students to break away from this mold and explore and to develop their gifts and talents at their own accelerated pace.

The belief that gifted education serves the privileged is not news to gifted educators; it remains as a powerful force undermining gifted programs today. The most common cry from detractors has long been that gifted programs are elitist. The ethnographic portion of the evaluation identified the historical roots of these charges of elitism. The negative reactions of parents and educators to gifted programs reflect a subtle paradox in American culture — the ambivalence inherent in democracy. Alexis de Tocqueville was one of the earliest analysts of American culture to recognize the dual nature of democracy. In *Democracy in America* (1899), he observed that "democracy breeds individualism" because each person progresses individually.

As the social conditions become more equal, the number of persons increases who, although they are neither rich enough nor powerful enough to exercise any great influence over their fellow creatures, have nonetheless acquired or retained sufficient education and fortune to satisfy their own wants. They owe nothing to any man, they expect nothing from any man, they acquire the habit of always considering themselves as standing alone, and they are apt to imagine that their whole destiny is in their own hands. (p. 586)

At the same time, de Tocqueville recognized the powerful force of conformity that democratic rule imposed on the individual: "In America, the majority raises very formidable barriers to the liberty of opinion: within those barriers an author may write whatever he pleases, but he will repent it if he ever steps beyond them" (p. 268). De Tocqueville wrote vehemently about the threat that this element of the American character offers. He characterized this side of American democracy as potentially more dangerous than the powers of a monarch.

The authority of the king is purely physical, and it controls the actions of the subject without subduing his private will; but the majority possesses a power which is physical and moral at the same time; it acts upon the will as well as upon the actions of men, and it represses not only all contest, but all controversy . . . . Under the absolute sway of an individual despot, the body was attacked in order to subdue the soul; and the soul escaped the blows which were directed against it, and rose superior to the attempt, but such is not the course adopted by the tyranny in democratic republics; there the body is left free, and the soul is enslaved. (pp. 267–268)

This fundamental contradiction in American culture between individualism and conformity provides the cultural backdrop for the political conflict surrounding gifted and talented programs. American parents strive to help their children achieve in an independent, competitive world by providing them with every available advantage. Parents of gifted children are the same in this regard — with one exception: They view gifted programs in much the same way that parents of a disabled child view special education programs — that is, as the bare minimum necessary to enable their child to succeed. Disabled children are often disenchanted with the conventional school system because they are overwhelmed. Gifted children are disinterested because they are not challenged by what the classroom has to offer. In either case, the result is the same: The students' needs are not met by the regular classroom curriculum. The obvious difference is that special education programs for learning and physically disabled children generally enabled the children to compete with their chronological peers, whereas gifted programs enable gifted children to move far beyond their peers. This discrepancy often provokes arguments in defense of individualism and egalitarianism, arguments often motivated by the democratic tendency toward conformity. Democracy in this case is defined as equality of ability rather than equality of rights — a view embedded deeply in the structure of the regular school system. In writing about the gifted child in American culture, Margaret Mead (1954) explained:

> If they [gifted children] learn easily, they have nothing to do; if they excel in some outstanding way, they are penalized as being conspicuously better than the peer group, and teachers warn the gifted child, "Yes, you can do that, it's much more interesting than what the others are doing. But remember, the rest of the class will dislike you for it." And there is in America today an appalling waste of first-rate talents, while the slightly superior people, just because they do have to work hard to get straight A's, are forgiven. (p. 213)

Moreover, Mead believed that American culture "tries to make the child with a gift into a one-sided person, to penalize him at every turn, to cause him trouble in making friends, and to create conditions conducive to the development of a neurosis. Neither teachers, the parents of other children, nor the child's peers will tolerate the Wunderkind" (p. 213). The response is logical and clearly embedded in American culture; however, in this case democracy has been confused with mediocrity (see Fetterman 1982, 1983).

Mythologies Supporting Neglect

"They Will Make It on Their Own"

Many people believe that gifted children have an inherent advantage in American culture. Their lack of contact with these students and programs generates half-truths and myths to combat perceived inequalities. One of the most persistent myths about gifted children is that "they will make it on their own."

Intellectually gifted students, by definition, are generally capable of learning more rapidly and on a higher cognitive level than their chronological peers. The regular classroom setting, as C. Switzer and M.L. Nourse (1979) point out, is geared toward the mean or average student. "The child is bombarded with forces which encourage modification of behavior, creativity, and intellectual development toward the mean of the group'' (p. 323). Consequently, the gifted child is rarely challenged in a regular classroom. According to Hollingworth (1942), an early investigator of the gifted, many gifted children learn to hide their talents to avoid ridicule or rejection from their peers, while others ''become contentious, aggressive, and stubborn to an extent which renders them difficult and disagreeable in all human relationships involving subordination'' (p. 261). In addition, teachers who resent challenging questions posed by gifted students subtly inform gifted students ''that their brightness, quickness is not as acceptable as the behavior of the less bright, more normal child'' (Jacobs 1972). Typically, these conditions give rise to academic underachievement and behavioral problems.

The myth that gifted children will make it on their own is even less credible when the children live in the inner city. Lemov (1979) has estimated that 30 percent of all school dropouts are gifted and talented. Gifted dropouts in the inner city, like those in upper-middle-class neighborhoods, represent a tremendous loss to our productivity and cultural development. The only difference is that dropouts in the inner city have fewer survival options than dropouts in the middle and upper middle classes in American society.

The U.S. Commissioner of Education's report on the gifted (1971) discussed the relationship between the lack of appropriate instructional environments for the gifted and high absenteeism, school abuse, and ''dropping out'' of school. The report concluded: ''Research has confirmed that many of the talented children perform far below their intellectual potential. We are increasingly being stripped of the comfortable notion that a bright mind will make its own way. Intellectual and creative talent cannot survive educational neglect and apathy'' (p. vii).

Elitism in America

A second myth is that the general education system does not foster elitist behavior. It is generally agreed that no other group, except for the disabled, is provided with ''preferential treatment.'' However, many groups of individuals with special talents or gifts receive encouragement to develop their potential and special treatment to achieve those aims. Roger Taylor (1980), a gifted and talented education consultant, provides an amusing story about another group that receives special treatment in the American school system. He assumes the role of a teacher attempting to ''sell'' gifted programs to the local board of education.

Good evening, board, it's so nice of you to have me come in to speak. I'd like to make a presentation here for the gifted programs in your district.

I.   I've decided that we ought to stop messin' around with the talented — let's go for the hard-core terminal gifted. I want to go for the upper one-half of 1 percent. Let's forget the nonsense about all this 5 percent stuff. I want the very, very best and let's not mess with the rest of them. Teach the best and shoot the rest.

II.   I really want to hire a gifted teacher. You've got to be gifted to teach gifted kids. I want to scour all over the United States. I want to find the greatest teacher who ever lived and I want to pay this person extra so we can really attract a superstar to work with these boys and girls.

III.   I want to build a special learning laboratory just for the gifted. I'm tired of gifted programs starting off in the janitor's closet somewhere. I want a special learning lab where we can showcase these gifted kids.

IV.   I want to have gifted carnivals for public relations purposes. Gifted carnivals where we could really show these kids off and they can show their stuff. . . . They'll [the public] be able to see how really good our school district can be when we have these very special one-half of 1 percent kids identified.

V.   Besides our gifted carnivals I want us to have gifted exchange seminars. For example, I'd like for the kids from your district to be able to go work at your state capitol where they could be pages in the senate. They could learn state government, while the kids from the state capitol could come and work at your district and they might be able to learn about urban problems or they might be able to work with solar and water conservation people — that kind of thing where we are able to move kids around.

And finally, besides our program exchange, I've been working out a logo for the United States. I'd like to be able to make some little brass belt buckles for the kids maybe with IQ on them or maybe some little badges in the shape of little brains that they could sew on their jackets and say gifted program.

And maybe for the summertime we could have some black t-shirts made up with a white fuzzy Guilford structure-of-the-intellect cube on the front.

A parent suddenly breaks into Taylor's school board presentation, screaming "You just stop it right there . . . that's the most anti-democratic, elitist, Marxist, hard-core communist nonsense I've ever heard of." Taylor explains at this point that he was not talking about the creation of a new gifted program; he was describing the existing gifted program: United States Office of Education category number six — "gifted psychomotor."

Let's go back to the outline. I. You've already identified the most elite population in any school district. It's not the upper 5 percent. . . . it's less than the upper one-half of 1 percent. You call it the first five on your basketball squad. You've already hired a very special teacher, a teacher more carefully screened than all the rest of the teachers in your entire district, probably more carefully screened than your school superintendent. And not only is this person carefully screened but he or she is paid extra so we can attract a superstar to come and work with these kids. Not only is the special teacher paid extra, but he or she also gets to dress differently. You always know the gifted program teacher, who wears color coordinated [uniforms], [a] whistle chain, matching Addidas . . . , and a stripe across the front [of the uniform] that says Coach.

I know you freaked out when I talked about building a special learning lab just for the gifted. Do you realize that, administratively, high school gymnasiums cost one-eighth as much as the entire physical plant all put together? And even though Moms and Dads had paid for that learning laboratory once with tax money, they still have to pay $1.75 to come in for gifted carnivals where we showcase the gifted. Oh, I'm sorry. You call them tournaments not carnivals . . . [this] is so you can finance your gifted exchange seminar program.

. . . All of the administrative hassles, all the logistics disappear into a thin vapor when it's category six gifted and we can take kids all over the state for round robin basketball games. All of a sudden insurance is no longer a problem.

And finally, VI. Some of you really chuckled when I talked about making little belt buckles. You were saying, well that's the most elitist thing I've ever heard of. He's talking about label-ing children. Well, but you see in almost any city in the United States I can walk down main street and spot the gifted a block away because they don't have little badges. They have whole jackets with white leather sleeves, black felt bodies, and great big letters that say varsity squad (Taylor 1980).

Taylor's discussion demonstrates how the American educational system fosters the development of an elite. Moreover, it illustrates how priorities are subtly established and how easily they are taken for granted. We may argue about the priorities involved, but we cannot deny that we do foster specific types of elitist behavior in our educa-tional institutions.

These and other misconceptions serve to mystify the gifted program and its participants and to further isolate them from the mainstream of the regular educational system. Moreover, these myths serve to diffuse the issue of the special needs of gifted children. Mead's words of 1954 still pertain today: "If it is true that we are at present lamentably poor in fostering genius, then it is obvious that we had better recognize what the obstacles are and proceed to clear them away. . . . [The sooner we face these] culturally regular myths about the desirability of normalcy . . . the better" (p. 213).

Overview

This book presents the status of gifted education on local, state, national, and international levels, with a focus on successful intellec-tually gifted programs in public education. There are, unfortunately, too many gifted programs in the United States and throughout the world that are gifted in name only. (See the Richardson study, Cox, Daniel, and Boston 1985.) This sad fact must be recognized and remedied. However, belaboring this problem distracts educators and policymakers from the larger concerns facing our educational system and thus the country. This book evaluates where we are as a nation without minimizing what has been done and what needs to be done in the field of gifted education.

Chapters 2, 3, and 4 are based on a three-year evaluation of one of the most comprehensive gifted programs in the nation — California's GATE program. Chapter 2 assesses the structure and function of the GATE program, which has served as a model for gifted programs throughout the United States. The program's administration is examined on the state level. In addition, the informal but significant administrative role of various advocacy groups, including the California Association for the Gifted, is explored. The driving force of the coordinator is presented on district and school levels. Two of the most salient characteristics of coordinators, examined on state and local levels, include political and charismatic dimensions of the individuals in these roles.

Chapter 2 also examines the cornerstone of any gifted program — the identification procedures. California has six gifted and talented categories: intellectual ability, high achievement, specific academic ability, creative ability, leadership ability, and ability in the visual and performing arts. The use of each category for the selection of gifted and talented children throughout the state is discussed. In addition, the fiscal and historical constraints affecting the selection of these categories are examined. The identification process is demystified by discussing each stage of the process, including search, screening, documentation, committee review, and identification and placement.

Finally, Chapter 2 presents an evaluation of the wide variety of programmatic approaches and grouping structures throughout the state, indicating the academic and political strengths and weaknesses of each approach. The premise underlying this discussion is that there is no single program or approach that can serve all gifted children. The most common program approaches and grouping structures in California are examined, including special day classes, part-time or pull-out groups, enrichment, cluster grouping, independent study, acceleration, and postsecondary opportunities. The adoption of a specific programmatic approach or grouping structure depends on the nature of the program's social and cultural context — the community environment. Calculating the impact of the communities' support for gifted education is instrumental in developing a program. Social and political insensitivity invites disaster. This section discusses how best to match programmatic approaches and grouping structures with community commitment.

Case studies are one of the most graphic means of presenting how gifted programs operate. Chapter 3 presents six case studies that capture much of the diversity observed throughout the state. These studies illustrate the richness and complexity of gifted programs. They include an elementary (all-day) pull-out program in a military community, an elementary cluster program in an inner-city magnet school, a secondary cluster program in a multiethnic low-income magnet school, a secondary cluster and seminar program in a multiethnic middle-class school, a secondary seminar program in an affluent community, and a secondary seminar program in a semi-urban community.

This chapter also explores and evaluates the role of values in specific gifted and talented programs. It demonstrates how program values can serve both as a source of strength and potentially as a source of program weakness. Adaptive values can produce a supportive and intellectually stimulating atmosphere and create community acceptance. Maladaptive values can destroy gifted children, poison their educational environment, and undermine community support. Adaptive and maladaptive practices are highlighted to improve programmatic practice in the future.

Chapter 4 is introspective in nature. Building on issues that emerged from the case studies presented in Chapter 3, this chapter addresses some of the most significant internally generated issues facing gifted programs today. The issues include the ethnic mixture of gifted programs, the IQ myth and the role of creativity in the identification process, the absence of theory in gifted education, attitudes and associations, psychological pressures, grading policies, and morality. These problems must be discussed openly and confronted. They will not disappear by themselves. Some of the problems strike at the heart of our democratic ideals. Facing them will help revitalize gifted education and, in turn, our entire educational system.

The GATE evaluation has implications for gifted programs throughout the United States. Similarly, in Chapter 5, a gifted program in Peoria becomes a national test case for gifted education and minority enrollment. This chapter represents a geographical shift from the West to the Midwest. Conceptually, however, the transition is slight because the issue of minority representation is the next logical step in this examination and evaluation of gifted and talented education. The Peoria gifted and talented program received national attention in the early 1980s for the same problem that plagues gifted programs throughout the world today — low minority enrollment. The controversy in Peoria revived old nature-nurture arguments, political battles, and personal animosities.

The evaluation of this program examined the program curriculum; instruction; the referral, identification, and selection mechanisms used; and the larger socioeconomic context of the program to explain the low minority enrollment. This test case demonstrated that low minority enrollment need not represent discriminatory practices on the part of the local school agency, nor does it support theories of racial superiority. In addition, this case demonstrated that the cause of educational problems often lies outside the classroom and in the community.

Chapter 6 represents a shift from local and national concerns to the international level. It presents a brief review of gifted and talented programs in nine countries. Gifted and talented programs reflect their own cultural and ideological context. The Soviet Union is able to circumvent its ideological barrier to gifted education by erecting an impressive network of extracurricular educational programs. Australia and New Zealand present an interesting contrast given their strongly egalitarian ethic. Many Australian states have been able to develop reasonable programs for the gifted in contrast to the paucity of programs available in New Zealand. Germany is still in its infancy in developing gifted programs, and in many respects its programs are an artifact of its existing educational system. Similarly, the cornerstone of gifted and talented education in England and Wales is part of their existing system — the sixth form. However, their programs in middle and secondary schools parallel programs in the United States in many respects. Canada, like the United States, Australia, and Germany, is composed of many states with many approaches to gifted and talented education, ranging from serious commitment to outright neglect. Israel's relatively new programs for gifted and talented children are extremely encouraging. Japan does not formally recognize gifted children; however, rigorous entrance examinations are required to enter high schools — which track students for college admission.

An underlying similarity of gifted and talented programs throughout the world is that they attempt to serve gifted and talented children in an egalitarian and hostile atmosphere — meeting the needs of both the individual and society at large. The focus in this chapter, and throughout this text, is on programs for the intellectually gifted child. Policies, programs, identification criteria, and curricula are examined. In addition, evaluative assessments are made whenever appropriate material is available.

The work concludes with a call to shake off our national complacency about the gifted and talented and to use this rich resource to restore our educational system. This chapter proposes a model of academic and administrative excellence for the U.S. educational system. The model is based on the best features of gifted and talented educational programs and on a synthesis of the preceding chapters. The elements of gifted and talented educational programs most worthy of emulation include quality, commitment, leadership, diversity of curriculum and instruction, and a whole-person approach. These features can be generalized to the mainstream of our American educational system. They can serve as guiding principles in the revitalization of our educational system.

We can accomplish this revitalization by first strengthening our gifted programs. The most important step is the reauthorization of a national center for the gifted and talented. A national center could refocus attention on the needs of this population and provide a sense of direction for teachers, students, and scholars in the field. Instructional materials could be developed and disseminated in a systematic and timely manner. In addition, exemplary projects could be encouraged and sponsored by a national center. Finally, a center could contribute to our understanding of the plight of the gifted and talented and help reduce the counterproductive hostility that has plagued the field since its inception. Such a national center could serve as a beacon for excellence in education for all nations.

CHAPTER 2

GATE Evaluation

California's Gifted and Talented Education (GATE) program has served as a model for gifted programs throughout the United States. This chapter provides a description and an appraisal of GATE administration, identification procedures, and programmatic approaches. It is based on the three-year evaluation of 433 gifted and talented programs in the state (see Fetterman and Wood 1982; and Wood and Fetterman 1981a, 1981b, 1983). This description and appraisal establish a baseline with which to measure other programs throughout the nation and throughout the world.

Administration

The superintendent of public instruction and director of education is responsible for the overall administration of the Gifted and Talented Education Program in California. The GATE program is part of the Division of Special Needs under the state's special education program.

The GATE Management Team is the state educational agency that is responsible for all pupils identified as gifted who are enrolled in gifted and talented education programs in the counties and districts of California. "The management team was formed to ensure that gifted programs would receive appropriate attention and high visibility" (GATE 1978). The management team is responsible for management, training, planning, evaluation, and development of gifted education research throughout the state. It is also responsible for coordinating activities with other state and federal programs. In 1981, for example, the team worked with Migrant Education Program staff to develop effective methods of identifying gifted and talented students within the migrant student population.

The management team was originally composed of three individuals. In 1982, one member of the team retired and has not been replaced. In 1983, the team's total operating budget, including salaries, was $118,546. The team's primary activities include screening all program applications, providing in-service training, and conducting program reviews. The time-consuming process of screening applications to ensure that they are feasible and that they meet state regulations appears to be operating smoothly, and there are only rare examples of programs out of compliance. In-service training is considered one of the team's most important services. The team shares new techniques, research findings, and information about new resources that may contribute to the state's gifted programs. These sessions also provide attending program staff members with an opportunity to share information and successful instructional techniques or curricula. Program reviews are conducted to certify that the programs are in compliance with state regulations and to offer feedback to improve individual programs. The reviews are thorough and range from classroom observation to budget audits. The tone of the reviews varies according to the composition of the review team. Personalities, local fiscal politics, and an assortment of other factors influence the program evaluations. In general, however, gifted education programs appear to appreciate the information derived from the reviews. The management team carries out an ambitious set of responsibilities, given its staff size and budget.

Advocacy groups are an informal part of the GATE management team. Although they are not technically a part of the state management of gifted and talented education, their power, influence, and resources rank them as some of the most important arms of GATE management. In California such groups include the Northern California Association for the Gifted (NorCal), the Pasadena Association of Gifted Education (PAGE), the Sacramento Association of Gifted Educators (SAGE), and the Association of San Diego Educators of the Gifted (ASDEG), among others. These groups are involved in developing and monitoring GATE legislation, policy, research, curricula, and fiscal affairs. The California Association for the Gifted (CAG) is the largest and most powerful advocacy group in the state. CAG is an organization composed of parents, educators, and professionals who advocate gifted and talented education. This organization provides both leadership and technical assistance on the state and local level. CAG represents a formal response to the opposition to gifted and talented education that exists on the classroom, community, and state levels. This organization has developed an intricate network of regional and statewide communication. Like other advocacy groups, CAG disseminates legislative, curricular, and administrative information about gifted and talented programs. In addition, CAG is a strong lobbyist for gifted education and has been characterized as a highly articulate vocal minority. Opponents of the program view it as a "thorn in their side," representing the only significant force preventing the legislature from withholding all funding from the program. CAG is also seen as the administrative hub of gifted and talented education in the state and is considered instrumental to the continued operation of the program on all levels. Members of the CAG board are aware that they are viewed by opponents and supporters as "coming on strong," but, as a former president of the organization explained: "We have had to fight for everything we have ever asked for. In other countries, the gifted are prized and encouraged. Only in the United States do we have to fight so hard for the rights of the gifted." Therefore, CAG represents an informal part of the management team and a formal organizational advocate of the special needs position for gifted children. (See Ballard 1984; Buescher 1984b; Coffey 1984; Fichter 1984; Gogel 1984; Jones 1984; Mitchell 1984; Monsun 1984; Sellin and Birch 1980; Wasson 1984; and Whitmore 1984 regarding the role of advocacy in gifted and talented education. See also Davis and Rimm 1985 concerning the role of the school board in this regard.)

The gifted and talented program coordinator is the driving force behind each of the individual gifted and talented programs operating in the state's school districts. These individuals are generally characterized as energetic, dedicated, enthusiastic, technically proficient, and resourceful, and they must possess these traits. Most of them occupy this position on a part-time basis: Approximately 62 percent hold this position for 25 percent (or less) of their time, and another 19 percent function in this capacity for 26 to 50 percent of their time. Their remaining time is allocated to other district responsibilities. Only 10 percent occupy this role full-time.

The most successful coordinators or leaders had one additional characteristic: charisma. Weber defines charisma as that "specifically exceptional quality" of an individual "by virtue of which he is set apart from ordinary men" (1968, p. 241; see also Bendix 1962, p. 88). Day (1980) defines charisma simply as "leadership with magic added" (p. 57). This special quality, combined with other administrative abilities, enables individuals to maximize the potential of an organizational effort, such as operating gifted and talented programs with few resources. In one case, where charisma and some degree of commitment were absent, the program lacked cohesiveness.

The primary responsibility of the coordinator is to supervise the district's gifted and talented program. The coordinator reports directly to the superintendent and must solicit the cooperation of individual principals in the district to implement the program. The coordinator usually has an informal influence and, in some instances, veto power concerning the selection of staff for the program.

This individual must be resilient, resourceful, and adaptable to changes or potential setbacks. Achieving many program objectives requires political acumen and skill in bureaucratic subterfuge as well. Supportive principals and school board members enable coordinators to achieve their objectives without using such tactics. Apathetic or antagonistic individuals, however, may severely disrupt program operations. Opponents of gifted education put a coordinator to the test. The successful coordinator attempts to accomplish objectives by circumventing such bottlenecks as uncooperative principals or by cutting bureaucratic red tape. Eisenstadt finds that charismatic authorities are "sharply opposed both to rational and particularly to bureaucratic authority. . . . Within the sphere of its claims charismatic authority repudiates the past" (1968, p. 51). Generally, however, the coordinator has initiated "good working relationships" with the school board, superintendent, and principal.

Weber (as cited in Bendix 1965) explains that a charismatic organization "is composed of disciples, chosen for their qualifications, who constitute a charismatic aristocracy" (p. 302). Day's study (1974) of a home for unwed mothers illustrates how such a relationship between the director and staff is essential to operating a program. Similarly, the gifted and talented coordinator's ability to select competent, dedicated, and effective staff members is critical to program operation.

The district coordinator is the link between the teacher, student, and parents in small communities. In larger districts, the school or site coordinator reports directly to the district coordinator. The site coordinator, in these cases, is a vital link in the administration of the program. This administrator is responsible for implementing the program on a daily basis. He or she is mediator and facilitator among parents, students, teacher, counselors, and administrators. The site coordinator in the largest districts that require site budgeting and planning has such complex responsibilities that the districts provide site management manuals. The strength or weakness of the coordinator — more than of any other individual in the GATE administration — determines the fate of the individual program. As a charismatic leader in a small organization, the coordinator has "the capacity to create and crystallize . . . broader symbolic orientations and norms to articulate various goals, to establish organizational frameworks and to mobilize the resources necessary for all these purposes" (Eisenstadt 1968, p. 39). The successful coordinator has a vision for the program, specific goals and objectives, and the ability to gather the resources required to accomplish those goals and objectives (see Alexander and Muia 1982; Gallagher 1985; and Newland 1976 regarding additional characteristics of gifted administrators).

Identification

The cornerstone of any gifted program is the identification and screening process. This component determines the shape and texture of a program. Criteria do not exist in a vacuum; they are contextual and cultural in nature. The criteria selected to identify the individual members of a group reflect the values of that group. A program designed for gifted artists will use criteria designed to reflect the appropriate disciplinary context. On a broader level, the criteria will reflect the cultural context. Identification tests are designed to select potential members of a group that possess the type of values and cognitive skills necessary for success in the dominant culture. American mainstream culture, however, is not a monolithic entity: Its values reflect the heterogeneous quality of American culture. This diversity, although skewed toward the dominant elements of the culture, shapes the categories and criteria for the identification of gifted and talented students.

GATE legislation allows districts to select their own identification categories and criteria within state guidelines. The six categories suggested are intellectual ability, high achievement, specific academic ability, creative ability, leadership ability, and visual and performing arts talent. The category of intellectual ability applies to students who demonstrate potential for extraordinary intellectual development, usually determined by group and individual intelligence tests. High achievement categorizes students who generate superior ideas and products and score exceptionally high on achievement tests.

Specific academic ability classifies students who demonstrate several years of advanced achievement in a specific academic subject and score well on achievement tests. Creative ability includes students who produce unique solutions to problems and test well on problem-solving examinations. The category of leadership ability is designed to identify students who display behaviors associated with superior leadership capabilities. The category of visual and performing arts talent describes students who possess superior capabilities in the arts.

Districts have most frequently selected for intellectual ability. There are a variety of reasons for the preponderance of intellectually gifted children in the program, ranging from historical to fiscal factors. First, the large percentage of students representing the intellectual ability category is partially a historical artifact. Approximately 48 percent of the GATE population is composed of former MGM participants, who represent existing students classified as intellectually gifted. New students in the intellectually gifted category constitute 27 percent; high achieving, 13 percent; specific academic, 5 percent; and the remaining categories of creativity, leadership, and visual and performing arts, 1.5 percent. Second, an effective curriculum already exists that is designed to meet the needs of gifted students in this category. A third reason for the large number of intellectually gifted children in the program is that instruments also already exist for measuring ability in this area. Last, a fiscal constraint that influences these figures is that the actual per-pupil expenditures have decreased since 1980. This decrease limits the degree to which a program can experiment with new gifted categories without reducing the impact of its primary approach.

Nevertheless, the percent of intellectually gifted students has actually decreased from 89.1 percent to 74 percent between 1980 and 1983. Moreover, only 30 percent of the new gifted students (50,271) were classified as intellectually gifted during this period. The remaining 70 percent of the new students entering the program between 1980 and 1983 are spread across the remaining identification categories. High achievement and specific academic categories represented the most statistically significant increases. This shift in context demonstrates the districts' commitment to experimentation and expansion in their definition and classification of the gifted child.

Local school districts are responsible for developing their own identification methods within state guidelines. These guidelines emphasize the significance of using appropriate technical standards and methods for identification as well as social standards; for example, they emphasize ensuring equal opportunity for students from various linguistic, economic, and cultural backgrounds (see Baldwin 1978; Clark 1983; Davis and Rimm 1985; Frasier 1979; Gallagher 1985; and Shade 1978 regarding the culturally diverse). The identification process is divided into five components: search, screening, documentation, committee review, and identification and placement.

The searching stage of the identification process is conducted pimarily by school personnel. Teachers and other school staff nominate students for the program. Unfortunately, teachers demonstrate an inconsistent ability to identify gifted children (Ciha, et al. 1974; Cornish 1968; Jacobs 1971; Borland 1978; Pegnato and Birch 1959; Gallagher 1966, 1985). Often the local gifted program will provide a list of key characteristics of gifted children to assist teachers in the search stage. Parents and students may also nominate candidates. (See Jacobs 1971 for accuracy of identification by parents.)

Screening is generally the responsibility of the district's school psychologist, who is responsible for reviewing existing data on candidates. Information may include scores on achievement tests, classroom grades, and/or special honors and achievements. The psychologist also receives the search lists from each school and is responsible for evaluating all nominated candidates. Group aptitude, achievement, and intelligence tests are often used at this point to more accurately assess the suitability of the candidate. The most common tests are the Wide Range Achievement Test, the Short Form Test of Academic Aptitude, the Peabody Picture Vocabulary Test, the Henmon-Nelson Test of Mental Ability, and the Lorge-Thorndike Intelligence Test. The psychologist compiles a list of students who receive superior scores on these tests. At this point, the district informs the parents that their child is a formal candidate for the gifted and talented program and requests permission for further testing. The more conscientious psychologists also solicit information from additional sources, including interviews with the candidates and reports from the students' teacher, counselor, and parents.

Documentation is also the responsibility of the school psychologist. Generally, the psychologist develops a case study of the candidate, according to the appropriate identification category. Building a case for assignment to the intellectual ability category requires student scores in the top 2 percent of the national norms on an individually administered intelligence test. This translates into a score of 132 on the Stanford-Binet L-M and 130 on the WISC-R test. Many districts simply rely on group-administered intelligence tests to defray costs associated with individually administered tests. Group tests are useful as a first-level screening mechanism; however, they lack the precision to accurately identify gifted children and should be complemented with individual intelligence tests and other measures. Some districts are flexible with the cutoff scores if the student has other compensating features that show promise. This can be a frustrating area for the psychologist confronting parents who are adamant about their child's inclusion in the program. Determined parents will have their child tested by psychologists outside the district until they score in the superior range. In some districts, this type of practice is prohibited. In others, determination depends on the individual will of the school psychologist and the parents. In all cases, various forms of subjective data are included in the file before the district makes a final assessment.

High achievement case studies vary throughout the state. Generally, however, the student must demonstrate achievement two or more years above grade level to qualify for this category. This is equivalent to stanine seven or higher on a districtwide testing with the Comprehensive Tests of Basic Skills. Other tests used include the Wide Range Achievement Test and the Peabody Individualized Achievement Test (see Hagen 1980 regarding limitations of abbreviated tests). In some schools, the high achievement category is used almost exclusively to identify "disadvantaged" gifted children. Achievement test scores are adjusted according to an "estimated deprivation" scale. Nondeprived students who score 130 or higher on the Wide Range Achievement Test are eligible for acceptance into the program, students with a moderate deprivation rating must score 120 or above to be eligible for the program, and students with a severe deprivation rating must score 115 or above to be considered for the program.

Specific academic ability case studies require demonstrated advanced achievement for a number of years in a specific academic area. In some districts, this type of case study requires superior student achievement scores (at the eighth and ninth stanine on the Wide Range Achievement Test), as well as samples of extraordinary student work. Districts that have adopted this category generally focus on areas in which they already have strong programs, such as math or English.

The remaining areas of identification, including creativity, leadership, and visual and performing arts, are still in the developmental stages. Currently, there are no nationally normed tests or standard operational definitions for these categories. Promising tests in the area of creativity include the Torrance Tests of Creative Thinking and the SOI Learning Abilities Test (see Tannenbaum 1983 for a discussion of these tests and others.). There is some debate about whether creativity should be taught in the abstract — separate from content-specific situations (Stanley 1980). The lack of clarity in this area is also evidenced by the absence of any clearly defined curriculum on the topic.

Leadership is a more nebulous category. Identification procedures generally involve nominations based on student government activities, social service leadership positions, and other civic organization positions of students already enrolled in the gifted program. Visual and performing arts is probably the most ephemeral of the remaining categories. However, it is the category with the most promise. The time and expertise of artists in the community are generally solicited to evaluate a candidate in this category. Often, the evaluator becomes the student's mentor as an adjunct to the regular program. (See Arnold 1977 and Stogdill 1974 concerning leadership characteristics and training.)

A committee composed of the school principal, an appropriate teacher familiar with the case, the school psychologist, and often a member of the GATE program reviews the documented case studies. The committee makes a determination about the student or a recommendation to the coordinator of the district GATE program. The final process of identification and placement requires unanimous approval of all members of the committee.

Programs — Curriculum Models and Grouping Structures

Teachers are clearly the most important part of any gifted program (Addison 1983; Bishop 1968; Renzulli 1980; Whitmore 1980). They provide coherence, continuity, and creativity in the classroom. The majority of gifted educators realize that no single program or curriculum model can serve all gifted children. There are, however, some gifted educators who have not recognized that the search for a single, all-encompassing gifted program is comparable to the search for the Holy Grail. The idea of a single program belies the fundamental tenet of gifted education — to serve the individual needs of the student. The Guilford/Meeker *Structure of the Intellect* model (Guilford 1967, 1977; Meeker 1969) and Renzulli's (1977) *Triad Enrichment Model*, combined with Bloom's *Taxonomy of Educational Objectives* (Bloom et al. 1956; 1964), represent the most influential set of curricular models used throughout the state. There are also a variety of other curriculum models available to meet the needs of individual students. For example, there is curriculum compacting (Renzulli, Smith, and Reis 1983), the "revolving door" approach (Renzulli, Smith, and Reis 1981), the "shopping center" orientation (Feldhusen 1980), Feldhusen's three-stage enrichment model (Feldhusen and Kolloff 1981), Stanley's (1980a) "smorgasbord" of alternatives, Treffinger's (1975) increasing self-directedness model, Taylor's (1978) multiple-talent pole model, Williams's (1970) thinking and feeling processes model, and various individualized models (Clendening and Davies 1980, 1983; Colon and Treffinger 1980; Treffinger 1981). Similarly, there is no one programmatic structure that is appropriate for grouping gifted children. Gifted programs do not exist in a social and cultural vacuum. The composition of the community — as well as the ethnic and cultural background of the students — must be taken into consideration in designing an appropriate program for gifted children.

The California Gifted and Talented Education program is composed of a large number of individual programs that are both diverse and complex in structure. Like any other program, it experiences difficulties. One teacher has said, "I think the best way to summarize this program is it's a utopia and as in all utopian-type concepts its greatest weakness is our human fallibility."

One of the greatest human weaknesses is hubris. Gifted programs often suffer from a false pride in their self-sufficiency and show little recognition of the interdependence of the program with the entire school system. The strength of any individual program, however, is inextricably linked to the health and vitality of the entire educational body. The structure of a program and the values of program participants and community members determine the fate of an organization's life, and a program developer must be sensitive to the impact of these factors. Many gifted program developers could avoid misunderstandings that result in polarizing the community by selecting a program that matches the community's commitment to gifted education. Insensitivity to the implications of program structure for organizational and community life invites disaster. A brief review of the variety of gifted programs operating in California demonstrates the significance of matching programmatic and community values. This matching process also helps to counteract hostility toward, and misunderstanding of, gifted education.

A variety of programmatic approaches or organizational structures to group students are used in the GATE program. There are full-time homogeneous classes, full-time heterogeneous classes, and a variety of part-time grouping programs. Programs are required to serve students for a minimum of two hundred minutes each week over a period of thirty weeks. The most common programmatic structures operating in California are special day classes, part-time or "pull-out" groups, cluster grouping, enrichment, independent study (with mentors), acceleration, and postsecondary-education opportunities. In practice, programs routinely use these approaches in combination. A brief review of the advantages and disadvantages of each approach underscores the necessity of adapting a program to the specific host community.

Special Day Classes

Special day classes are composed entirely of gifted and talented students who are brought together for at least one complete school day. Students may come from throughout the school or throughout the district, depending on the size of the program. Special day classes may be conducted one day a week, a few days a week, or throughout the entire week. The length of the program is a measure of the community's commitment to gifted education. The selection of this type of program is also a function of the size and experience of the district. Districts with over thirty thousand students enrolled generally have special day classes on the elementary level. Approximately 17 percent of the elementary GATE student population and 5 percent of the junior and senior high school GATE student population are served by these classes.

Special day classes generally represent the most effective approach to meeting the needs of gifted children, enabling gifted children to work and socialize among their intellectual peers for at least a full day a week. Many students refer to this special class day as the "one day in the week that I look forward to." Gifted students in our study often complained that their regular classes were boring and that they were not encouraged to present novel ideas in the regular classroom. In the special day classes, they were encouraged to express themselves. As one student said: "You get to use your imagination. You're not afraid to say anything. There is no right or wrong answer, only your opinion, but they make you support it. At the regular school it's all right and wrong answers. At the regular school you just sort of suffer through it. Here you like it."

One of the most significant weaknesses of the one-day-a-week special day classes is that they lack continuity. These classes rarely have homework, and, since they only meet once a week, a teacher must complete the entire week's lesson in one day. He or she must also provide the student with a sense of closure each time they meet. This approach often prevents the in-depth exploration of a subject that teachers and students expect. In addition, it regularly removes the students from their everyday class. The regular classroom teacher may interpret this removal as disruptive and as an infringement on teaching time. In these cases, the teacher may become resentful and increasingly insensitive to the gifted students' additional work loads. In several reported cases, the regular schoolteacher required the gifted child to make up both the classroom work and the homework for the day, in addition to the special day activities. This was required even in situations where an "agreement" existed between the regular school and gifted program, absolving the gifted student of the responsibility for completing regular classroom homework on the special day. Gifted children often interpret this behavior as being directed at them personally. It is an unresolved power play in which children lose. The gifted child rarely complains about this type of problem for fear it may jeopardize his or her enrollment in the program. One gifted student in this type of program explained: "We know we are not supposed to have to do this [the regular classroom work] but we want our teachers to like us and it's not hard so we just do it to stay in this [the special day] program."

The special day program that operates full-time each weekday eliminates many of the problems related to the one-day-a-week approach. The key to the success of this type of approach is peer competition and program continuity. Grouping students with similar skill levels often enables them to compete in a fashion that challenges them. This competition can shake them out of a sense of complacency and enable them to produce consistently high-quality work. This approach enables gifted students to work at their own pace with their intellectual peers on a regular basis. In addition, teachers can provide a program that has continuity. Students are no longer confronted with boring classes and resentful teachers, and can explore each subject in greater depth and engage in long-term educational projects and activities. A sustained period of time to concentrate on a topic enables students to progress at a geometric rate, as compared with briefer and more sporadic periods in which to focus energies and talents. In any case, the special day option requires a supportive school administration, qualified teachers, and a politically astute, gifted coordinator.

One of the disadvantages of this approach is that it isolates the child from the rest of the school population. Students who have participated in these programs throughout elementary school have reported in high school that they believe they "have missed something." Many gifted programs attempt to encourage their students to become involved in other school activities. This involvement is generally fostered, however, at the high school and junior high school level — after much early childhood socialization has been completed. Many of the things that students feel they have missed are basic socialization skills with chronological peers — that is, knowledge of their social interests and participation in their activities.

Most important is the fact that this isolation of gifted students provides the best target for charges of elitism. Regular classroom teachers and parents have little understanding of this type of program because it operates independently. Myths develop about the program out of ignorance, for example, that "it's all fun and games." In addition, resentment builds up; regular teachers think that gifted teachers are getting the best children and incorrectly assume that they are receiving additional compensation for teaching these classes. This type of program is highly visible and is easy for parents and others to identify. Vocal parents are quick to bring up the issue of equitable educational treatment. A common question emerging from this situation is, Why are those students receiving preferential treatment and my students are not? This type of question quickly leads to discussions of elitism and egalitarianism. The problem can be ameliorated through greater integration with regular programs and a carefully cultivated campaign for local administrative and community support. Nevertheless, the structure of this programmatic or grouping approach makes it an easy target for such attacks and as such requires continual communication with the school and community that house the program.

Part-Time Grouping

Part-time and cluster groups are the most common approaches adopted by California GATE programs. Part-time groupings are more frequently observed at the elementary level than are cluster groupings, and are often referred to as "pull-out" programs. Identified gifted and talented students are removed from the regular school program and grouped together for part of the school day to attend qualitatively different classes or seminars. This type of program offers a minimum of qualitatively different instruction and usually operates in a community that offers minimal support for gifted education for fiscal or ideological reasons. The approach does offer the student a brief opportunity to explore problems in more depth or to become involved in a more engrossing advanced activity, for example, dramatic performances. However, most individuals associated with this approach, such as the coordinators, the gifted teacher, and the regular teacher, characterize it as "frustrating and highly disruptive," requiring the most effort from a gifted teacher. Since these gifted teachers are often hired to work exclusively with gifted children, their link to other educators and to the administration is weakened. In addition, the gifted teacher must spend much time scheduling the student to attempt to minimize disruption and must "run around" each day from school to school like a traveling salesperson. It is not uncommon for part-time grouping teachers to have their office and supplies in the trunk of their car. Echoing a general complaint, a teacher said that "little can be accomplished with this type of schedule." Moreover, students are rarely able to recall what was discussed or accomplished in these sessions.

A successful program depends on the creation and maintenance of a strong link between the gifted teacher and other schoolteachers, the administration, and the students' parents. A special dash of altruism is also essential: This type of instructional and coordination time is rarely compensated. Fundamentally, the problem with this approach is that it is part-time, whereas the gifted child is gifted full-time. As the Richardson study (Cox, Daniel, and Boston 1985) concludes: "It is a model whose time has come and gone. A serious drawback is the false sense of accomplishment it can provide a district; it is easy to establish such a program and believe that the needs of able learners are being met" (p. 44).

Cluster Grouping

Cluster grouping is used to serve the largest percentage (48 percent) of GATE students on the secondary level. The use of this approach on the elementary level is second only to the adoption of the part-time grouping approach. This approach clusters or mixes gifted children with high achievers in the same classroom. However, they are usually identifiable as a cluster to the trained observer or educator. Gifted students remain in the regular classroom, and special instruction for the gifted is provided by the regular classroom teacher. This instruction is supposed to be qualitatively different. Ideally, the teacher provides differentiated levels of instruction for gifted children and high achievers, with contracts for independent educational activities or independent study programs. (See Davis and Rimm 1985, pp. 116–117). There are many advantages to using this approach. Scheduling problems that arise from part-time grouping are eliminated, and costs are lower. This approach requires no extra expenditures of funds over and above those that the district would expend without the program, although teachers are generally required to complete gifted certification or in-service training. In addition, this approach is one of the few economically feasible ways to serve the gifted population in a district with few identified gifted children. Another significant advantage is that it eliminates the problem of isolation and the concomitant charges of elitism that result from special day or homogeneous grouping. Gifted students are intellectually and socially exposed to a broader segment of the school population, that is, to high achievers. This exposure has a number of benefits for the various parties concerned. Gifted students who are underachieving are often challenged by high achievers and motivated to compete more vigorously to fulfill their potential. High achievers can benefit from exposure to a higher level of discourse and effort than is afforded them in the regular classroom. In addition, a wider range of teachers and students come in contact with, and become knowledgeable about, program materials and activities. This contact serves to demystify the program.

The most significant problem with this approach is that it can be easily replaced by a regular honors or advanced placement class. District manuals explicitly state that gifted classes are not to substitute for these honors classes and that they must be appropriately differentiated learning experiences. High schools, however, are independent agencies operating in the district. The operation of a gifted program is dependent upon the local principal's commitment to the program. A qualitatively different program can exist using this approach only when the coordinator, principal, and teacher demonstrate their commitment.

Enrichment

Enrichment activities are usually combined with other approaches. In its most positive form, students remain in their regular classrooms and are provided with advanced materials or special opportunities designed to supplement their regular educational program. The exclusive use of this approach indicates a lack of district commitment to gifted education. Generally, however, when this approach is used in conjunction with special day classes, part-time grouping, or cluster grouping, it becomes an essential part of the program. It enables the student to become exposed to a wide variety of activities and materials that are qualitatively different from their regular instruction, for example, oceanography, theatrical performances, museums, literature, and so on.

Independent Study

Independent study serves only a small percentage of gifted students — approximately 6 percent at grade eleven and 7 percent at grade twelve. It may involve receiving instruction from a mentor or enrolling in a correspondence course. Typically, however, independent study involves working with a teacher on a course designed by the student. This approach, like enrichment, is most useful when combined with other more substantive approaches; it then provides the freedom to explore an area of interest or strength not provided by the regular school program. Coordinators often help establish an independent study program for a student by arranging a match between a mentor in the community and a gifted child. Mentors in the GATE program have included physicians, social scientists, artists, musicians, Nobel Prize–winning physicists, and writers. This approach exposes gifted students to a number of individuals and topic areas that are pertinent to their own interests and development. In some cases, after being intensively exposed to a field of endeavor, students decide not to enter a specific area of study. This is also a useful learning experience: Elimination of certain lines of inquiry based on actual experience helps students learn how to make important decisions about where they will direct their talents. Generally, however, independent study programs provide a student with an avenue to explore areas of interest or expertise free of the conventional constraints of a regular classroom.

A disadvantage of this approach is that it offers insufficient guidance or instruction unless it is combined with another, more encompassing approach, for example, special day classes or cluster grouping. In addition, it is difficult to arrange the match between a community resource person and a gifted student. Scheduling logistics and identification of appropriate mentors are time-consuming processes. Mentors outside the educational community require training and guidance to properly fulfill their roles. This approach also relies heavily on sustained student motivation, and many gifted students have difficulty maintaining sufficient motivation to complete independent study endeavors. One student in a group conference expressed the sentiments of the group in the following way: "It's great to have the freedom, but if there's nobody over you, it's easy to slip back and take advantage of it." This approach works best when the appropriate match is made between mentor or teacher and student. The student must be highly motivated and should take the major role in designing the course. The mentor or teacher should allow the student as much freedom as possible to pursue the study but should still provide guidance and a "watchful eye" over each of the student's tasks (see Boston 1976; Davis and Rimm 1985; Gallagher 1985; Gray 1984; Sellin and Birch 1980; and Tuttle 1978 regarding description, guidelines, and benefits of the mentor approach; see also Cox, Daniel, and Boston 1985 concerning the differences between a mentor, intern, apprentice, and assistant, pp. 59–74).

Acceleration

Acceleration involves placing students in grades or classes that are more advanced than those of their chronological age group. *Grade skipping* is the classic method of acceleration. *Subject skipping* involves acceleration in a subject area and is often referred to as "partial acceleration." *Telescoping* involves condensing or collapsing the high school program into two or three years. Acceleration is more frequently used on the secondary level than on the elementary level. Accelerated students also receive special counseling or instruction outside the regular classroom to facilitate their work.

The issue of horizontal or vertical movement usually emerges in discussions of acceleration. One school may promote vertical movement or acceleration, while another may advocate horizontal growth or enrichment. There are advantages and disadvantages to either approach; in any case, students should not be accelerated to the exclusion of enrichment. The independent variable most frequently used to determine whether a student would benefit most from acceleration or enrichment is maturity. If the student, parents, counselor, and teacher decide that the student is mature enough to work productively with his or her chronological elders, the student is advanced vertically. If, however, the student is ready for additional qualitatively different work and lacks maturity, he or she is generally provided enrichment. There are, of course, a number of other variables that are taken into consideration, such as the parents' desire that their child experience all the social activities associated with his or her age group, the level of potential advancement involved, and the child's feelings. For many students, acceleration is either the best or the only alternative available in a school system. Research strongly suggests that acceleration is a valuable approach in educating gifted and talented children. However, most school systems are extemely reluctant to use the acceleration approach. As Gold (1965) states, "No paradox is more striking than the inconsistency between research findings on acceleration and the failure of our society to reduce the time spent by superior students in formal education" (p. 238). (See Stanley 1980a, 1980b; and Stanley and Benbow 1982 regarding benefits of acceleration in mathematically precocious youth. See also Begle 1976; Eisenberg and George 1979; Elwood 1958; Gallagher 1985; Gold 1965; Goldberg 1958; Gowan and Demos 1964; Justman 1954; Klausmeier 1963; Kulik and Kulik 1984; Mirman 1962; Reynolds, Birch, and Tuseth 1976; and Ripple 1961 regarding the positive results of acceleration.)

Postsecondary-Education Opportunities

Finally, postsecondary-education opportunities are usually offered to gifted high school students for some portion of the school day. Approximately 13 percent of the GATE students at grade eleven and 26 percent of those at grade twelve attend college or community college classes during the school day. The most important advantage of this approach is that it allows the student to grow at his or her own pace and, in some cases, to advance through the educational system more rapidly. In addition, this approach exposes gifted students to a wide variety of course offerings not available in high school, including computer programming, statistics and advanced mathematics, and sciences. Serious problems can occur if the students are not emotionally prepared for the pressures of college life or if the college lacks a supportive mechanism to help students adjust to college life. (The University of Washington's Early Entrance Program is exemplary in this regard.) Minor difficulties, such as transferring credits, can also occur if the administrative details are not thoroughly investigated before the student enters the college or community college (see Davis and Rimm 1985 for a discussion of this and other models and grouping structures).

Conclusion

The GATE program is dependent on a multilevel administrative structure that exists from the state level to the individual school level. Informal networks and support groups also strengthen GATE administration. Identification categories are varied, but all categories focus on intellectual or special ability in practice. In addition, numerous curriculum models and program grouping structures are available throughout California to serve the needs of gifted children. The type of program in operation is often a function of community support or neglect. Program developers need to examine the match between programmatic approach and the social and cultural context of the community if they are to serve the gifted and avoid unnecessary hostility

The next chapter provides a closer look at specific programs — and focuses on the values that shape daily behavior. Case studies highlight the adaptation and maladaptation of functioning programs. The detailed pictures of these programs provide the data with which we can analyze the basic features of these gifted and talented programs.

CHAPTER 3

GATE Case Studies:
Underlying Values

A program's values are at once a source of strength and a source of potential destructiveness. Case studies offer a graphic depiction of the role of values in the gifted and talented program. Two elementary schools and four secondary schools have been selected to demonstrate program variation. Full-length case studies were used in the ethnographic evaluation of the GATE program. They have been condensed and presented below to illustrate the dynamics of gifted programs and to portray the experiences of a few gifted students. The discussion of values that follows crystallizes some of the problems common to several programs.

Childrens' Academy

Childrens' Academy is an elementary school (all-day) pull-out program. There are three sessions, each approximately ten weeks long. Students attend one day a week — fifth grade on Monday, sixth grade on Tuesday, second and third grade on Wednesday, and fourth grade on Thursday. Fridays are used for planning. Most students at Childrens' Academy come from highly mobile military families. As a result, the school has a high student turnover rate. Classes are taught by two gifted and talented teachers and the district coordinator. Since they are taught simultaneously throughout the day in a single unpartitioned room, teachers and students have learned to adjust to the volume level and the tight quarters. They work effectively within their groups without interfering with the other groups. The curriculum is divided into four topic areas: science, math, social studies, and literature and fine arts. The coordinator attempts to ensure that each student participates in each of the four areas throughout the year.

41

GATE instructional objectives include a wide range of intellectual, psychosocial, and study skills. The program's instructional objectives correspond to lists of materials, activities, and evaluation procedures. Gifted teachers take students' preferences into account when assigning them to given courses. Interesting titles are used to attract students to available courses, such as "Money Makers," "Build a Better Mousetrap," "The World-Go-Round," "Weather in 3D," "Shipwrecked," "Sleuthing with Sherlock," "Blood and Guts," and "Reading Between the Lines: Magic, Myths, and Morals." Some parents are concerned that there may be too much fun and games in the classes. Meeting with the coordinator and observations of classroom activity, however, have clarified the depth and purpose of these courses. The classes involve problem solving, navigation, meteorology, biology, poetry, and so on. "Blood and Guts," for example, is biology with a focus on anatomy. Students in this course participate in activities such as taking their pulse every morning, learning about human anatomy, and dissecting animal hearts and brains.

I participated in the dissection class during one of my visits to this program. A young "military brat," as he referred to himself, befriended me for the week-long visit. Robby is a very small fourth grader, highly verbal, and clearly eager for attention. He followed me everywhere, wearing a military camouflage hat. When the time came to begin the dissection, the instructor had a limited number of cow hearts, so Robby and I teamed up and worked on one together. We both took notes from the lecture, read the literature, and followed the dissection guide on the board. When I found the left ventricle, I showed Robby my great discovery; when he found the fibrous tissue, he shared it with me enthusiastically. After the first fifteen minutes, I let Robby discover the intricacies of the heart by himself. The teacher had only allocated half an hour for the dissection, but Robby and most of the other students were mesmerized by the experience and chose to keep working. The dissection class ended two hours later than planned. This level of intellectual and emotional immersion was typical of the gifted students observed throughout the programs.

Each day, the Childrens' Academy program ends with an affective-domain social-skills session. For example, the classes are divided into three-person teams. Each student in a team presents a one-minute autobiography to his or her team members. The students are told that they will discuss what they learned about their peers afterward. This exercise develops group speaking and listening skills. These sessions are also useful for developing general socialization and maturation skills. For example, in one triad, a gifted student born without arms volunteered to discuss his handicap and his perception of the difficulty people have in accepting him as an individual — a problem he considered a greater impediment than his physical difference. The students appeared to learn from and appreciate their opportunities in the Childrens' Academy GATE program. One student echoed the sentiments of several others: ''Tuesdays are something to look forward to now. At school we just get the basics; here they let you think.''

The teachers have also implemented an effective assertive discipline technique (Canter and Canter 1976) to encourage cooperation, politeness, and creativity and to discourage discipline problems. The technique involves positive and negative reinforcements. Students are given awards for ''good'' behavior, such as helping another student on a project, working through part of lunch on a project of interest, improving the rate of attendance, and so on. Similarly, students are denied opportunities to attend extracurricular activities and their parents are contacted if disruptive and nonproductive behavior becomes a pattern. This system guides the entire program. Program rules and expectations are clearly communicated, and reinforcements are distributed promptly and appropriately. Students and parents expressed uninhibited and unsolicited praise for the program — during school hours, at GATE and district meetings, and in their homes. The students' attitudes toward the Childrens' Academy were summarized by one of the younger students: ''Here it's okay, you enjoy it — at the regular school you have to tough it out.''

Alhambra Elementary

Alhambra Elementary is a magnet school. Magnet schools are usually inner-city urban schools that have been selected to receive special funds and programs to attract students from throughout the city. In this case, the city is using magnet schools as a tool to initiate a voluntary desegregation plan. Alhambra is in a low-income, predominantly black and Hispanic community. Many parents from the suburbs have decided to bus their children to this school to take advantage of both the math and science program and the gifted program.

Alhambra has cluster gifted classes from kindergarten to grade six. The cluster classes involve math, English, and science at two or more grade levels above that of comparable regular classes in this school. In addition, various enrichment activities are available to the students, ranging from special guest lecturers to field trips.

The seminar part of the gifted program involves grades three through six. These students are taking advanced courses, learning to program personal computers, and pursuing various other educational activities. One of the more impressive elements of the seminar program at Alhambra is the publication of the elementary school newspaper. Gifted students from grades three through six write, edit, paste up, and print the paper. The articles are well written, clear, concise, and relevant to both students and staff. In addition, the students sell advertising space to local merchants. Students in the fifth- and sixth-grade gifted classes also produce television news on the school's closed circuit television. The students write scripts for, act in, film, and edit all broadcasts. Students from the regular classrooms are always invited to participate in the production.

Gifted students at Alhambra are leaders and competitors in many school areas. They are typically school representatives for the annual Science Fair, and they are also very active in sports. The program has produced a long list of student accomplishments, ranging from winning national academic competitions to artistic achievements. During my last visit to this program, I met Gary, a young, black student who had been identified as academically gifted. He had never played a musical instrument before coming to the program. In the gifted program, however, every student is required to learn to play the piano and to acquire some knowledge of the basics of musical composition. Gary began playing immediately and was playing concert pieces in less than three and a half months. This kind of discovery results as much from the program's expanded opportunities as from the child's inherent ability.

Alhambra Elementary's administration is highly supportive of its gifted program. The gifted program teachers and the principal have been close friends for many years. This tightly knit relationship has enabled participants and planners of the program to experiment, develop, and expand over the years — regardless of the city's fiscal problems. In 1983, however, the program came under attack from local community members. They were enthusiastic about the quality of the program, but enraged about the program's racial mix.

Local community leaders accused the principal and a few gifted education teachers of being racists. Alhambra uses the same identification criteria as the rest of the district; however, it has not been able to identify more than a handful of gifted minority students. The principal explained the dilemma as follows:

> In the past, minority students have been brought into the program — without being identified and without the requisite skills for the program — to satisfy community pressures. The[se] students soon fell behind the rest of the class. They became frustrated and asked to be sent back to their regular class. The parents are the ones that get shook up. They respond antagonistically, with comments like "You said my child was gifted last year, now you're saying he's not!"

This practice has created frustration among children and resentment and bitterness among parents. The principal and the gifted program teachers also feel handicapped by school district and city administration policies and procedures in their efforts to recruit qualified minority students. The gifted program teachers complained that the only money available to bus students into a magnet (minority) school was allocated to white students to provide a better racial balance. The teachers explained that this practice made it difficult to bring minority gifted students from other parts of the city into the program. The community outcry had reached such a pitch at that time that the school principal, who planned to retire in one year, was transferred to another school by downtown administration.

Alhambra's gifted program still receives strong support. Gifted program teachers, however, fear that local leaders will abuse their new powers and use the program to their own advantage as a rallying point for any racial issue. Gifted program and regular teachers in the school were concerned that this type of behavior might severely damage the integrity of the program in the future.

King High School

King High is a magnet school located in a multiethnic, low-income community. The gifted program, when successfully used, attracts students from across the district to promote integration. It has cluster grouping and serves students in grades seven through nine. The program also has special classes for highly gifted students in grades seven through twelve. Subjects include English, science, social studies, history, and physics. The physics class is taught by a credentialed teacher in secondary education with a Ph.D. and ten years of experience in the aerospace engineering industry. She left the aerospace industry because she "wanted to work with human beings, to prepare these kids, to teach them how to cope with change." As she says, "Life is change." This teacher is committed to interdisciplinary studies; for example, she uses exercises in poetry to demonstrate right- and left-brain function. On the day of our visit, she introduced a physics lesson on sine waves by playing harp music and then discussing the dynamics of the music in terms of basic principles of physics.

Many GATE students in King High School are accomplished in various areas. One GATE student has conducted extensive award-winning research on neurofibromatosis, the disease that disfigured England's John Merrick, the Elephant Man. Another student began studying laser holography in eighth grade and later constructed his own reflection and double beam transmission holograms. This student won first place in a physical science state fair. Recently, his research has resulted in the production of a holographic movie — an accomplishment matched only by a few optical scientists in the world. A third student (a junior) taught herself differential calculus during the 1981 summer vacation and has won numerous state awards for her mathematical research. Other students have been involved in restoring an old twelve-inch Newtonian reflector telescope that was donated to the program. These same students have conducted "deep-sky observation as well as astrophotography." Tenth-grade physics GATE students wrote, produced, and acted in "The Meeting of the Masters," a play dealing with the lives of Shakespeare and Galileo, and they performed this play at a local science theater. Thus King High School's gifted students have eclectic interests, ranging from spiritual subjects to astrophysics; however, their primary focus is summarized in the following adventuresome student's remarks: "I enjoy conversations about religion with the Krishna — it's like lots of fuzzy pretty colors. But I like the white light of science best."

Dublin High School

Dublin High is in a middle-class, multiethnic community. The school has 1,500 students, 210 of whom are enrolled in the gifted program. The acting vice-principal is a former gifted teacher. The gifted classes take place in a cluster and a two-hour-a-day seminar program. The physical appearance of the seminar program makes it visibly distinct from the rest of the school program. Couches encourage a relaxed atmosphere. A personal computer allows students to learn programming skills, although computer games are strictly prohibited. Independent work centers enable groups of students to work together on various projects. The double-sized classroom has a "lived in" look, as one student characterized it. The principal uses the terms *messy* and *cluttered* to describe the papers and clothing strewn about the room. The physical atmosphere is of an informal, hard-working, independent classroom, and observations and interviews confirm this impression.

The seminar class is taught by two gifted teachers, one responsible for English and the humanities and the other for science instruction. The English and humanities teacher has been in the program for many years and has worked with the founding teachers of the present gifted program. She is highly dedicated and has written district manuals about gifted curriculum. Her class consists primarily of assigned readings, analytical discussions, and individual and group papers. Topics throughout the year include current literature, medieval literature, the work of Shakespeare, poetry, the nineteenth-century novel, and twentieth-century literature.

During one of the second-year site visits to the English and humanities seminar classes, students were observed discussing the role of metaphor and epiphany in Joyce's *A Portrait of the Artist as a Young Man* and preparing papers based on ideas developed in these discussions. In the third year, I observed a co-teacher lecturing on the life and works of Turgenev to an eight o'clock Monday morning cluster class. For the first half hour, most students were struggling to stay awake. This part of the session was characterized by a typical lecture note-taking orientation. By eight-thirty, the students' response and the nature of the discussion had shifted dramatically. The teacher asked about one of Turgenev's characters: "Why is he so rude? He goes home and immediately insults everyone. What do you make of this character?" The students responded in force and in depth to this unassuming question. One student said the following: "I think it's good. He's kind of fallible, he's not perfect. . . . Once he's brought down to the human level, as it were, you see him as a full person. Somehow, he becomes more endearing and believable." A second student explained: "It seems like he's a typical teenager. A young person that doesn't like the establishment. He is rebelling. Then later he is calm." A third student built on this statement: "It seems like when people are young there are many things they don't like. They don't like what the government does and when they get older they accept it more. I don't know if that's good, but that seems to be what happens." The teacher linked these thoughts back to the novel to guide the discussion. The students slowly took control of the discussion and drew comparisons between Steinbeck's naturalism and Turgenev's realism. Characters of various other authors were dissected and compared. The role of historical context was introduced into the discussion as the bell rang. The teacher brought some closure to the discussion and explained that it would continue during the next session. Some students lingered after class, arguing about the validity of various points that emerged during the classroom session, while others continued the last part of the classroom discussion with the teacher. A few left the classroom immediately to attend their next class. Generally, the cluster class was marked by a high level of discourse in the humanities.

The other half of the program focuses on science instruction. This instructor has only been in the position for one year, or since he replaced the last instructor, who is currently the acting vice-principal. This present instructor teaches primarily out of a college textbook. He has not had time to set up a laboratory, and no steps have been initiated to secure access to school laboratories. He is also currently an executive officer of the local branch of a national educational association, a position that demands that he spend much of his time defending other teachers who are in conflict with the administration. In addition to taking time away from his work in the gifted class, this role periodically places him and the program directly in conflict with regular school faculty and administration. Parenthetically, this instructor has agreed to vacate his position, recognizing that the program requires a full-time commitment. The screening process for a new instructor will take these factors into consideration.

The students enjoy the science seminar class and indicate that they have gained much from the class, more than they receive in their regular classes. They do complain, however, that they would like a laboratory and would like more classroom activities. They also complain of isolation. For example, one student in the seminar class explained: "For me, one of the problems of this program is that most of my friends are in here and I don't take people in my outside classes that seriously. I don't put myself out as much to make friends with them." Similarly, a more extroverted student in the gifted class, who is on the school football team and is involved in various other school activities, explained: "I think outside involvement in school activities becomes very important when you get in a program like this because you can become very isolated." This close-knit group, however, has many advantages for a gifted student. It affords students with intellectual similarities an opportunity to engage in stimulating conversations and to explore areas not discussed in regular classes. One of the social advantages this group provides is "safe harbor" — a place where one can be oneself, temporarily free from outside peer pressures and hostilities.

Gifted students in the program experience some regular teacher hostility. This problem exists for many reasons: Some teachers think the program is undemocratic ("all students should receive the same education"), others believe the best students in the school are being "taken away" from them, and still others believe that students in the gifted program are lazy — are "being given a free ride at the taxpayers' expense." Site visit observations, however, revealed a qualitatively different level of discussion, writing, and experimentation with ideas in this class compared with regular classes in the school. The classroom is best described by two students in the program.

1st student: I would draw the analogy of a womb.
2nd student: I think that's a very good idea because if you look at the fetus in the womb it's just kind of quiet but really, there is a lot of growth going on and people on the outside don't really understand how much work is really being done in here. My friends say, "Oh, you're in [the gifted program], you're lucky you don't have to do any work." I say, "I'll give you some of my books."

Overall, the students and teachers in this gifted program believe that some improvement is needed, but they are satisfied with the general approach. Moreover, a strong personal bond has been established between teachers and students in this program. One of the students explained this relationship in an idealized manner: "I don't think of her as my teacher or my counselor, I think of her as my friend. We have discussions about literature, but we can also go to her when we are bugged by something or when we need our schedule changed.''

Trinity High School

Trinity High is in an affluent professional community. The school population is approximately 1,300 students, 100 of whom are in the gifted program. Approximately 80 percent of school graduates enter institutions of higher learning. The principal is highly supportive of the program, and the vice-principal is actively involved in establishing the seminar program in the district and is deeply committed to the program. The community is also very supportive of the program — intellectually, emotionally, and fiscally.

The multidisciplinary gifted course offers advanced English, advanced world history, advanced American literature, and advanced U.S. history. A two-hour, two-teacher seminar program exists for gifted students in grades ten through twelve. The physical atmosphere of the seminar room, like that of Dublin High, distinguishes it from other classrooms in the school. Three couches add to the room's comfortable ''lived in'' look. A personal computer room and a few additional features reflect the wealth of the community. A portable color television set in the room allows students to watch midafternoon news. A small stage for dress rehearsals is adjacent to the seminar room.

One teacher in the seminar program is extremely traditional, and the other is considered more liberal in her teaching style. In practical terms, the traditional approach translates into lecturing, testing, and an authoritative demeanor. The liberal approach involves values clarification, discussion-oriented lessons, reports, and self-evaluations. The students enjoy the contrast and explain that ''they [the teachers] complement each other well.'' They combine sessions and defer to each other when one teacher requests additional time with the students on his or her topic area.

During a third-year site visit to this seminar class, I observed the students using a college literature text to discuss Flaubert's *Madame Bovary*. An active discussion was taking place regarding the main figures in the novel — Charles and Emma. Charles was characterized as ''a happy man'' because he was simple, compared to Emma, who would never be happy because of her complexity and her passions. The students analyzed various passages that followed this theme and made comparisons to other authors in the same genre. One student concluded: "It is interesting that the main tragedy in realism is not being able to deal with realism." The discussion was continued during the next session with the same enthusiasm and search for answers to the philosophical issues raised in the novel. Another literature class focused on the tutor and the tyro in Steinbeck's plays. Class discussions in the seminar program were engaging and intellectually stimulating. Students openly shared their interpretations and insights and were also highly critical of unsupported views. The teachers primarily served as facilitators, supporting and guiding the discussions. They also assigned numerous readings and routinely tested the students on their understanding of the curriculum. Teachers also served as assistant directors for the plays that gifted students in the seminar program performed throughout the year.

These students often do not fit in regular classes. One student explained, "When I get bored with a class, I only do enough to get a B." Another student continued, "When I get bored with a class, I don't go." Clearly, some regular teacher hostility exists toward the gifted program. Many of the teachers in this school are extremely well-trained professionals who believe that they are not being given an opportunity to work with the "cream of the crop." In one case, the hostility resulted from an individual teacher's insecurities and a gifted student's impatience and impertinence.

> Everybody was talking in the class and walking around. I couldn't get any work done, so I decided to leave to go to the library. The teacher told me to stop. I said, "What for, everybody else is just walking around and talking," and he said, "Just sit in your seat." I decided to walk out anyway. He said I would get a referral. I just said, "If you can't run your class without pulling this authoritarian insecurity thing, then you are no teacher and call me when you start to change" and I walked out of class. Well, I got a referral and a transfer to a lower-level math.

This student was able to complete the work; however, he was unable to cope with an irrational and authoritarian situation. His motivation was reduced in other classes, and other gifted students who have known him for a number of years explain his current behavior in the following manner: "He is existentially opposed to the school system. It's not that he is lazy." Fortunately, few teachers display such open hostility toward gifted students in the program, and most gifted students have learned to cope with irrationality in the classroom and to work effectively with authority figures.

A congenial atmosphere exists in the program. One student explained: "It's sort of a family. We might sit around on the couch. It does get to be a small town, everybody gets to know what everybody is doing. It also has a family feeling. So there is the good and bad. You're not a nonentity." Students explain how the teachers "are not just teachers." They say: "They are people you can go to. If you have a problem you can talk to them and it's really a very trusting relationship. . . . They respect you." Students are generally extremely supportive of each other; however, they can also be extremely sarcastic toward one another. In fact, as one student explained, "There are incredible opportunities for inferiority complexes in here" as a result of the keen intellectual competition. Students in this specific program are highly pressured to enter the best universities in the country. In fact, one of the teachers expressed the opinion that only Ivy League and a few West Coast schools were acceptable schools for his students. One student said the following: "Their whole attitude, the whole time, is that you're not doing enough. You're not doing enough for yourself. There's always more that you can do and . . . they always expect you to do that. They push you to do as much as you can to fulfill your potential." Another student explained how the program differed from his other classes: "In the other classes, you do the work that they assign you and if you do it then you're done, and here you don't, you have to do more, you're never finished. In most classes, you're graded against the whole class, the curve. [In this class] you're graded against yourself." The pressure to produce scores required to enter college is appreciated by the majority of students interviewed. They realize that this is preparation for more than college. Joan explained: "It's not just college that they're gearing you toward, but intellectual life." Regarding parents, another student explained: "Our parents are a little more overbearing and supportive than the average parent. They will say, 'why can't you get an A in that class,' but they will then go out of their way to help you."

The program occupies only two hours of the day; however, all of the gifted students in the program are enrolled in the same advanced honors courses throughout the day. This situation can lead to a maladaptive, segregated life-style that is not conducive to the student's social development. One student complained, "We are isolated in this room, in an isolated school, in an isolated community." This isolation can produce prejudices among gifted students toward students in the regular school program. This problem was highlighted in a lighthearted but sarcastic discussion about interacting with students who are not part of the program.

John: You've got a group of people with, well, I don't like to say this because I don't like measuring people's intelligence . . .
Phyllis: If you're going to be elitist, just go out and say it.
John: I find it interesting to talk to other people but . . .
Sue: To see how stupid they are. [laughter]
John: To find out what they're like, to find out what they feel like.
Barbara: [You mean] "What does it feel like to have an IQ of 87?"
John: Okay, you're being hard on me.

This type of "teasing" among gifted students is rarely, if ever, revealed to outsiders. Barbara's intention was primarily to chastise John in a lighthearted manner for his taboo — but commonly held — beliefs about other, regular students. The discussion, however, revealed a condescending attitude toward regular students. Gifted students in some exclusively gifted programs are socialized to interpret their "special qualities" as a form of superiority. Although they are rarely in mixed company for long periods of time, they learn not to express these attitudes openly. Parents are also concerned about these attitudes and push their children into other activities to ameliorate this problem, for example, into sports, clubs, and mixed classes.

Parents are also concerned about other issues, such as how acceleration or enrichment might affect their children. One set of parents decided not to accelerate their fifteen-year-old child into a college program because they believed that "there are other things in life. We made a family decision about this because there are other things like sports, baseball, and dating, not just academics." Parents of gifted children are generally highly supportive of their children's education. In one case, the parents moved halfway across the country to enroll their child in this exemplary gifted program. In addition, they are extremely vocal advocates of the program and appreciate the gifted program teacher's contributions to their children — both academic and personal. One parent provided an example of how his child had problems juggling dating, sports, and classes. He then explained how one of the teachers helped his son establish his priorities and how he "got him back on track" saying, "It was no small accomplishment what he did and we appreciate it." In another example, a parent described how her child was becoming increasingly "distracted." He would be "soulful and dreary" in the regular honors classrooms. Mr. Oxford (one of the gifted teachers) reorganized this student's schedule. As the parent said: "My son had had a problem organizing his time. Mr. Oxford had David come to school at 6:00 a.m. every morning to plan his day. After a short time, David was getting A's again. These teachers are dedicated. They are firm and loving in ways I couldn't be."

Oasis High School

Oasis High is located in a semiurban community. The school was a victim of white flight several years ago, and the white student population has dropped from 54 to 34 percent. This school experienced much upheaval during the transition. However, students appear to be working together in a compatible manner.

The gifted program at Oasis is a seminar program. The two-hour-a-day class is entitled "Intellectual, Cultural, and Social History." The course covers major themes that have emerged from and characterize Western civilization. The course includes lectures, guest speakers, classroom discussions, class projects, films, extracurricular activities, reports, and essay tests. J.P. Morgan, the teacher, completed his doctoral studies at Stanford University. He is also independently wealthy and has made a conscious decision to pursue the life of a high school teacher as his avocation. He has adopted a variety of qualitatively different approaches to teaching his course. Nazi death camp survivors are guest speakers in the World War II section of the course to provide additional depth and insight into a "war like no other." This approach has been used repeatedly to emphasize the value of firsthand accounts and original documents in historical research. A film of the bombing of Hiroshima introduces students to "the dawn of the atomic age." Moreover, this emotionally disturbing film is used to provide the dramatic context of all World War II conference treaties. The film presents a realistic demonstration of the threat of world destruction that shaped the conditions and language of these treaties — and of all major arms agreements from that time to the present. A third part of his course covers the 1920s and 1930s in American history. Morgan is a stickler for historical accuracy and requires his students to learn the slang of the period during this part of the course. In addition, one of the major projects in the course is the full-scale replication of a Tea Dance — with appropriate apparel and a live band playing music of the period. No plastic materials are used, since they were not invented at the time. The full-dress simulation of this 1928 Tea Dance involves proposals for work plans, rehearsals, and construction efforts during lunch and after school. These efforts take place in addition to normal classroom readings, examinations, and reports. These projects evidence a student and teacher commitment beyond the normal school obligations. Moreover, this type of team effort serves to develop a sense of commitment and group cohesion that are generalizable to other projects.

Morgan stresses writing skills and uses lengthy essay examinations as part of his course to prepare students for college work. Essay questions range from the ramifications of Nobel Prize lectures to the historical basis and significance of specific (unidentified) political quotations. Morgan is a popular teacher. He is, however, a "hard grader." The only criticism students made was that he graded on a curve. Morgan explained that he adopted this type of evaluation system to prepare his students for the realities of academic life. Students, however, are aware of the relationship between grades and college entrance requirements. In fact, a few gifted students have dropped out of his class out of fear that they would receive a lower grade for work that would be highly evaluated in a regular class. In general, however, most students believed that the course was "worth the risk."

Conclusion

These condensed case studies help to portray the role of values in shaping gifted programs. Values can strengthen and guide gifted programs in a productive fashion. Teachers who adopt a firm but supportive approach toward educating the gifted and talented can produce a climate that fosters a desire to learn and explore. High expectations and explicit standards of excellence challenge students and contribute to the caliber of classroom work and discussion.

Recognition of the fiscal and political values of the community enables the program to survive.

Conversely, values can serve to undermine the efforts of the best gifted program. Insensitivity toward program selection and hostile community attitudes toward the gifted can be extremely harmful. Similarly, ignorance on the part of program administrators about the larger political climate in their community can place a program in an unnecessarily vulnerable position. For example, failing to acknowledge charges of elitism or racism can be lethal. Such charges — whether valid or invalid — can bring any program to its knees.

Well-intentioned but misguided value systems also damage a program. Parental, teacher, and peer pressure to perform, for example, can paralyze the efforts of the most promising student. In addition, an ignorant and insecure teacher may disillusion and alienate a gifted adolescent. Furthermore, isolating the gifted in separate programs — without any contact with regular students — can produce socially maladaptive behavior and reinforce such problems as egocentricity and misperceptions about nongifted students. (See Gallagher 1985 concerning societal values and their impact on programming.) The following chapter builds on this discussion by abstracting many of the issues found in these case studies. These critical issues are of concern to programs not only in California, but across the nation and throughout the world.

CHAPTER 4

GATE Revitalization

Revitalizing a movement and an organization requires hard work. Many areas require attention in the restoration of gifted education. The most significant areas that emerged from our study include the ethnic mixture, the IQ myth, the absence of theory, attitudes and associations, psychological pressure, grading, and morality.

The Ethnic Mix

An important social and political responsibility of any gifted program is to have a reasonable mixture of ethnic groups. The old MGM program was narrowly represented — in both ethnic and talent categories. The state expanded the categories to be served under the AB1040 legislation. In addition, it said, "The legislature finds and declares that it is in the public interest to support unique opportunities for high achieving and underachieving pupils . . . from economically disadvantaged and varying cultural backgrounds" (California State Department 1979, p. 2). Gifted and talented program staff have generally accepted the bill as a welcome improvement to the program. Although legitimate concerns exist about the ability of the program to expand its criteria without an increase in funding or a reduction in quality, the overall response to this bill has been positive.

On another level, this legislation represents an equitable resolution to charges of elitism. An expansion of the talent categories and a greater representation of ethnic groups potentially broadens the base of the program sufficiently to meet the majority of vested interests in the taxpaying population. Advocates and detractors both agree that broadening the base of the program — in terms of talents and ethnicity — is vital politically to the program's continued existence. Consequently, the ethnic and talent mix was one of the critical areas monitored during the three-year evaluation. All parties were interested in the extent to which the program could implement the new legislation — which would probably be the extent to which it could answer the charges of its most passionate opponents in the debate over special need versus special privilege.

Unfortunately, as is the case for the majority of gifted programs nationally, proportional ethnic representation was one of the program's weakest areas. At the time of the study, white and Asian groups were overrepresented in proportion to their size in the student population. Whites represented 52.5 percent of the student population and 70.8 percent of the GATE program. Asians represented 6.3 percent of the student population and 10.4 percent of the GATE program. Hispanics and blacks were underrepresented in proportion to their size in the population. Hispanics represented 27 percent of the student population and only 10.2 percent of the GATE program. Similarly, blacks represented 11.7 percent of the student population and only 6.4 percent of the GATE program. Filipino representation was proportional. American Indians and Alaska ı natives were only slightly underrepresented.

To be fair, these figures must be placed in perspective. Schools are continually being asked to solve social problems, and they can either be change agents or promote the status quo. Unquestionably, schools have a role to play in the social arena; however, their power should not be overestimated. The discrepancy between the representation of ethnic groups in the larger student population and that in the GATE program mirrors larger social and economic discrepancies in our culture. The burden of proportional representation cannot be placed solely on the shoulders of the educational system. Many social problems must be addressed before we can realistically expect to see dramatic changes in our schools.

In addition, research and funding must be improved. Insufficient research is being conducted on the relationship between different subcultural cognitive styles and learning patterns and gifted and talented program identification practices. The type of tests required to accurately identify gifted children from all ethnic and cultural groups has not been designed. The instruments and methods used to identify gifted children still reflect the dominant or majority culture. The GATE program has also suffered a decrease in its per-pupil funding. On the average, the state provides $13.28 less per pupil in the program than it did three years ago. Therefore, requirements to expand identification categories and programmatic approaches and to achieve proportional ethnic representation while reducing the program's real dollars are unrealistic. Gradual progress in such a constrained fiscal and cultural context represents a real achievement.

Societal expectations for our schools do exist regarding fairness, equal opportunity, and specifically proportional representation, even though we have not adequately dealt with questions of ethnic and racial equality as a nation. The gifted and talented program clearly needs to be improved to meet these expectations; however, some accomplishments do exist in this area. A long-term perspective reveals that these population figures show a real change in the ethnic mix over the three years in which the program was evaluated. There has been a 71.4 percent increase in the numbers of Filipino GATE students enrolled in the program (from 1,840 to 3,153). A 45 percent increase has taken place in the numbers of Hispanic GATE students enrolled in the program (from 12,390 to 17,998). A chi square test indicates that this group (Hispanics) had the most statistically significant increase in the program. Asians increased 33.9 percent, blacks 21.7 percent, and whites 15.3 percent. American Indians and Alaskan natives actually decreased their enrollment in the GATE program by 1.9 percent. Excellent gifted education programs in other states find these figures enviable. A program in another state consistently reported four-tenths of 1 percent black students in its gifted and talented program, yet blacks represented 40 percent of the third-grade population from which gifted program participants were drawn. The program is currently being threatened with termination of funding because of its representation problem. This program will be examined in detail in the next chapter. California's and other states' programs face funding difficulties and potential termination if more dramatic changes do not occur in their ethnic composition.

The IQ Myth and Creativity

Myths and half-truths are often perpetuated by outsiders. However, potentially damaging myths are also generated from within a group, often out of pride and ignorance. The most common function of a myth, in this regard, is to distinguish a group from the outside world.

One of the most dangerous and misleading myths perpetuated by the gifted program itself is the equation of IQ with giftedness.

The identification process is dominated by group and individual intelligence or IQ scores. But IQ scores do not measure intelligence, only a narrow spectrum of this psychological construct. Moreover, as a tool, the IQ score is inappropriate for grouping students for instruction. As Stanley (1980b) points out:

> Using only IQ or MA scores to group pupils homogeneously for instruction in mathematics is foredoomed to be inefficient compared with grouping based on more relevant criteria.
>
> This points up the need for frequent use of tests or other assessments of special abilities that, singly or in combination, provide a more valid basis than IQ for instruction of youths talented in a given school subject. (p. 8)

Currently, scores are used more often to label students than to diagnose and prescribe curriculum needs. In addition, teachers, parents, and gifted students have complained for years of the narrowness and consequent imprecision of this instrument in the identification process and in curriculum development. Classifying a child with an IQ score of 130 as gifted while leaving out the child with a score of 129 is arbitrary. One student explained: "I don't like the overemphasis on IQ scores for admission into this program. I know many students who scored well but do not belong in this program. Conversely, I know many students who did not score well enough to enter the program — but they are gifted."

A more poignant concern is expressed by minorities who fear that these tests are being used to screen them out systematically from educational opportunity (see McClelland 1973). Different cultures have different conceptions of intelligence and different ways of manifesting that conception (Baratz and Baratz 1970; Berry 1966; Cole et al. 1971; DeLeon 1983; Dorset 1970; Vernon 1969; Witkin 1979; Witkin et al. 1974). Tests are culture bound. As Davis and Rimm (1985) state:

> These traits, of course, are based upon middle-class English. The problem is that subcultural languages such as black English (Baratz 1974; Labov 1974), Hawaiian pidgin, Navajo or other Native American languages are different and so the person's linguistic structures, categories and associations are also different. Group intelligence tests depend heavily on language ability and therefore are more likely to be biased than individually administered tests. (pp. 260–261)

Minority groups are legitimately concerned that tests reflecting the dominant culture put them at a competitive disadvantage. Moreover, there is a fear that these tests may be misused. They bring to our attention the time in American history when these cognitive ability tests were used to discriminate against Polish, Italian, and Jewish immigrants. A 1912 U.S. Public Health Service report concluded "that [intelligence] tests establish that 83 percent of the Jews, 80 percent of the Hungarians, 79 percent of the Italians, and 87 percent of the Russians were 'feeble minded.' "

The danger of overemphasizing the value of IQ scores is further emphasized by the conclusions of various scholars about the poor correlation between these scores and adult success (Munday and Davis 1974; Harmon 1963; Helson 1971; Helson and Crutchfield 1970). Clearly, efforts are needed to balance the role IQ scores play in the identification process. For example gifted programs need to take into consideration concepts of creativity, motivation, and other characteristics in the identification process (see Tannenbaum 1983). Creativity is often thought of as a critical characteristic of the gifted child, and it is routinely addressed in the classroom. In the course of the three-year evaluation of the GATE program, however, we observed little attention to the identification of "creative/productive giftedness" (Renzulli 1982). Approximately three-tenths of a percent of gifted children were identified under the creativity classification. In many respects, creativity is an elusive characteristic (see Khatena 1971, 1973; Treffinger 1980; Treffinger and Poggio 1972; Treffinger, Renzulli, and Feldhusen 1971; and Wallach 1970). Nevertheless, Renzulli describes creative and productive giftedness as "those aspects of human activity and involvement where a premium is placed on the development of original material and/or products that are purposely designed to have an impact upon one or more target audiences" (1982 p.12). Creativity tests need to be refined and improved, and also need to be tested for reliability and validity. As Tannenbaum (1983) explains: "To say that an instrument's predictive validity has not been disproven conclusively is a long way from confirming that it is valid. The burden of proof is with the test constructor, and subsequent research should supply further support of data. These conditions remain yet to be met consistently in research on creativity" (p. 280). National norm testing is required. There are, however, many useful measures of creativity, biographical inventories, and guidelines for the identification of creative children that programs could begin to use today (see Guilford 1966, 1967, 1973; Merrifield, Gardner, and Cox 1964; Rimm and Davis 1980, 1983; Rimm, Davis, and Bien 1982; Torrance 1966, 1974; Torrance, Khatena, and Cunnington 1973; and Wallach and Kogan 1965). These tests, inventories, and basic clinical data are needed to balance the current statistically myopic view toward gifted identification. As Treffinger (1982) explains:

Clinical sources of information are those that are personal, individual, and qualitative in nature. Statistical data are primarily quantitative. In gifted education, our concern should be to mature beyond a preoccupation with quantitative or statistical data alone, recognizing that the most effective psychoeducational planning may prove to be that which successfully synthesizes the statistical or quantitative evidence with the clinical or qualitative evidence. (p. 21)

The IQ myth and a preoccupation with statistical forms of identification are fostered from within the program. Greater flexibility is needed in the process of identifying gifted children. Renzulli (1982) points to a model already in the schools:

Basketball coaches are not foolish enough to establish inflexible cutoff heights because they know that such an arbitrary practice will cause them to overlook the talents of youngsters who may overcome slight limitations in inches with other abilities such as drive, speed, team work, ball handling skills, and perhaps even the ability and motivation to outjump taller persons who are trying out for the team. As educators of gifted and talented youth, we can undoubtedly take a few lessons about flexibility from coaches! (p.12)

The Lack of Theory

One of the least discussed but most glaring holes in gifted and talented education is the lack of theory. No overarching theoretical framework exists for the development of gifted and talented programs. The absence of a theoretical base makes the development of gifted and talented programs a vulnerable and shaky proposition at best. Theory informs practice and provides a framework in which to help students develop. Without such a framework, a specific gifted program may show little relationship between a given curriculum and the development of intelligence. In other words, there may be no long-term merit to a program's educational treatment. This situation applies equally to all forms of education. Educational programs and research are dominated by fads, and educational research rarely provides conclusive proof that one "treatment" is superior to another or that treatment A caused effect B. Nevertheless, an attempt should be made to base curriculum and program developments on a strong foundation.

Alexander (1984) makes a strong case for adopting cognitive theory as the basis for the design and development of gifted and talented programs. She describes how information processing as one of many intelligence theories may have "the potential to mold many of the developments in gifted education into a more consistent, coherent structure." One of the most promising subtheories in the field is being developed by Sternberg and Davidson (1983). Their information-processing approach "emphasizes processes in insightful thinking"(p. 52). There are many intelligence theories that could guide program development. The problem in gifted education, as in other educational areas, is that these resources are being ignored — without any regard for the impact on student development.

Many successful programs have been explicitly and implicitly influenced by the work of Bloom (Bloom et al. 1956), Guilford (1967), and Renzulli (1977). In lieu of an explicit theory, programs could benefit from these models and approaches. Bloom's system includes six levels of cognitive activity: knowledge, comprehension, application, analysis, synthesis, and evaluation. Gifted programs that have adopted Bloom's approach have structured their curriculum to enable students to engage in progressively higher degrees of intellectual interaction. Guilford's three-dimensional model of the structure of the intellect divides a cube into 120 cells defining specific intellectual factors. The model involves five kinds of operations: cognitive, memory, divergent production, convergent production, and evaluation. It also includes six kinds of products: units, classes, relations, systems, transformations, and implications; and four kinds of contents: figural, symbolic, semantic, and behavioral. Many gifted programs have developed diagnostic and curriculum materials based on Guilford's model of the structure of the intellect. The Structure of the Intellect Institute has created a diagnostic test that measures many of the separate intellectual abilities proposed by Guilford (see Meeker 1969). Workbooks and prescribed worksheets have been designed to remedy weaknesses and build upon the strengths of individual students, as indicated by diagnostic testing. Renzulli's cognitive model has three levels. In the first level, teachers serve as facilitators. In this stage students are encouraged to clarify their own interests and abilities. The second-level students learn how to work in a group. This educational relationship helps the student master the content of a specific area. In the third stage, gifted students are encouraged to adopt scholarly methods of inquiry to investigate a particular area — individually or in groups. Renzulli suggests that the first two levels of activity are appropriate for all students and that the third level is the major challenge specifically designed for gifted children. These useful approaches are not meant to serve as replacements for the development of sound theory. They are, however, excellent interim measures in shaping gifted and talented programs.

Attitudes and Associations

The problem of elitism has been discussed from a cultural and theoretical perspective. The basis for this problem can also be found in the day-to-day activities of gifted and talented program teachers and coordinators. Although district coordinators set the tone for a district, the site coordinator and individual instructor define the actual shape and characteristics of a gifted program. Moreover, school faculty members develop their attitudes about gifted programs on the basis of their interaction with gifted program personnel. The individual personalities, idiosyncrasies, talents, and associations of gifted staff members, therefore, shape school faculty perspectives on the program. In other words, each gifted and talented teacher and site coordinator serves as a representative of the program.

In general, gifted and talented personnel are dedicated and responsible representatives of the program. In the few cases where antagonisms are visible and charges of elitism are openly made, the problem can be traced to individual representatives of the gifted program. The problems range from individuals who misuse the program as a cultural status symbol to misplaced political affiliations. A minority of instructors are more concerned with maintaining an image of a cultural elite and exclusively serving white upper-middle-class students than with planning, preparing, and performing activities to serve all gifted children. These individuals shed a poor light on the program. In addition, instructors who visibly align themselves with and immerse themselves in political activities and associations like ROTC and NEA often endanger the program, since regular faculty members' attitudes toward the program are generally shaped by the gifted teachers' political affiliations. Guilt by association is unfair, but it is a practical reality. Although personal and political preferences cannot and should not be mandated, gifted teachers and coordinators work in a highly political and vulnerable environment and must be aware of how their activities affect the program.

Psychological Pressure

A more encompassing problem confronting gifted children is the psychological pressure to achieve. Gifted students establish extremely high standards for themselves. Parents, teachers, and peers compound this problem by setting additional standards (see Krueger 1978 for gifted students' perspective on these pressures). Parental pressure is probably the most pervasive and subtle influence on gifted students (see Davis and Rimm 1985 regarding parenting gifted children). One student said, "My father is a geophysicist and so he never verbalizes it but you know that if you didn't go to one of these top schools, boom, that would be it." Another student demonstrated the significance of parental pressure in her life:

I have internal motivation at times. I also know that if I did poorly my parents wouldn't be happy. I've gotten a C before, in 9th grade, and my mom just said, "This isn't very good, this isn't nice." You know when your parents are disappointed in you it's the end of the world. Now I could never get grades like that but I know that if I did poorly my parents would be upset. They want me to go to a good school. They have security in mind.

Teachers are also a crucial motivating force. Their high expectations force students to achieve, but this motivation is a double-edged sword, since their expectations add to the psychological pressure to achieve that the gifted child feels. One student described this process:

He [the gifted teacher] does put more academic pressure [on us] than [the regular teacher]. Specifically, he will express his disappointment in your performance more than [the other teacher] and you will feel that and in a way it does supplant a parent, a parent figure. If you do poorly and get a bad score he will say, ''Look at this, this is not good enough and we are going to nail this one down next time.'' He will ask you if you need a tutor. You then feel forced to do it.

The standards that result from these well-intentioned and useful pressures are often unrealistic. In fact, teachers and students have reported a few cases in which these pressures have been demoralizing for gifted students.

The perfectionist syndrome is a commonly reported problem among gifted students (see Whitmore 1980, pp. 118–124, for a case study example of paralyzed perfectionism; see also pp. 145–147). Perfectionists often withdraw from even simple tasks if they fear that they cannot meet the standards that they pose for a given task. Moreover, gifted students often equate academic achievement with their personal identity. Academic error is often translated into personal failure. This identification may manifest itself in a number of ways. For example, a student may drop out of the program, or, as we observed during one of the last site visits, a gifted student serving as a volunteer docent may apologize profusely for an insignificant factual error made during the tour. In one case, a group of gifted students asked whether it was true that ''you could only go to Stanford, Harvard, Princeton, or Yale'' to be successful in life. Other students were observed making self-deprecating comments about themselves for minor errors in tests, experiments, or class discussions.

Two basic types of pressures are experienced by gifted learners. The first is the pressure imposed by gifted learners and others to achieve — to enter a good school. The second is the burden of the label *gifted.* Teachers are often intimidated by gifted learners. During a recent site visit, comments such as ''You're supposed to be bright, you can figure it out yourself'' were heard in regular classrooms with gifted students. Nongifted peers also maintain stereotypes of the gifted. One young gifted child explained, ''I find that most people stereotype us people in [the gifted program] and automatically if you're in [the gifted program] you like computers, you like Dungeons and Dragons, you're weird, you're a freak.'' Another student reported a contrasting stereotype: ''people [other nongifted students] think you sit around on the couch, you know, doing nothing all day, taking advantage of the program.'' These complex and often damaging psychological pressures represent the context in which the gifted learner functions in school on a daily basis.

One of the most useful mechanisms to reduce these pressures is peer association. Gifted students are relieved to learn that others have similar problems and solutions. As one student explained, ''It's a lot easier to get along with [other gifted students] because they understand you.'' It is in fact ironic that one of the contributing sources of competition — peers — is also one of the most powerful antidotes for peer pressure. Generally, we observed gifted students helping each other personally and academically.

Grading

Grading is probably the most significant area in which the psychological pressure to achieve and compete manifests itself. This problem is compounded by the fact that there is no systematic or uniform grading system for students in gifted and talented programs. The curriculum and the evaluation of pupils are usually left to the discretion of the individual teacher — within the overall guidelines and requirements of the district. In general, teachers and students who used the mastery system, in which the student is only in competition with himself or herself, appeared satisfied with the grading process. A few problems with the current nonsystematic approach, however, were reported and observed during the last site visits.

One problem with evaluating gifted pupils involved grading on the curve. In this instance, gifted student scores are distributed across a bell-shaped curve. This system sets limits on the number of pupils that will receive an A,B,C,D, or F. In this case, a student might receive a low grade in the gifted class, whereas he or she would have received a superior grade in a regular or honors class. This difference causes problems because students and parents take the ''college game'' seriously, and often students decide to drop out of the more challenging gifted program to receive an easy grade. Similarly, we observed classes where students received a C for performing at the 100 percent rate of their grade level because they were expected to perform beyond their grade level. These students quickly became disenchanted with the gifted program and potentially with the educational system in general. In both cases, the problem of dropping out is twofold. First, these students are no longer pursuing a program that challenges them to fulfill their potential. Second, teachers and students report "sinking down to the same [academic achievement] level" of their peers. For example, one teacher explained: "I had one boy drop out of the class because his parents were concerned about his chances of making it into the Ivy Leagues. They figured he'd get straight A's in regular honors courses. But he's getting average grades now — B's and C's."

A more commonly observed problem in evaluating gifted and talented students is the converse of the previous examples. The overwhelming majority of gifted students observed received automatic A or B grades for their work. Students reported enjoying the freedom, explaining that it allowed them to pursue their interests without external pressure. Most of those interviewed, however, suggested that it was easy to take advantage of this evaluation system. One student explained: "When you're motivated, it's great, you really get a lot done, there's nothing to get in your way. But then when you're not [motivated], you're not, and it's easy to just slip back and do nothing for a while. " The automatic A or B grading system, like grading on a curve, does a disservice to the gifted student, since it does not prepare students for the rigor of college work. In addition, this system can promote underachievement by rarely challenging students. Its only advantages are that it releases the gifted students from some of the college game pressures and that it serves as a safety net to catch troubled and disoriented gifted students.

The attitudes and approaches under discussion often inhibit gifted students from fulfilling their potential. A blanket grading system, like a blanket gifted curriculum, is not appropriate or feasible. Too many different types of programs, teachers, and gifted students exist to produce a uniform system. Some boundaries, however, should be established to identify appropriate and inappropriate approaches. In addition, systematic guidelines should be developed for the use of various types of student evaluation systems. Assigning a C to a student who has completed 100 percent of his or her grade-level work, for example, should be considered outside the boundaries of acceptable student evaluation methods. Debatable areas involve grading on a curve and automatic A grade assignments. It has been argued that grading on a curve realistically prepares students for college work. The problem with this argument is that it assumes a homogeneous population. A gifted class is an atypical composition of students who represent a small academic range of variation. College classes generally comprise a much wider variation of students than do gifted classes — from a strictly academic perspective. The majority of gifted students can be expected to perform at a high level that would be on the end of a bell-shaped curve in college classes. Grading on a curve, therefore, does not realistically prepare gifted students for college-level evaluation. In fact, this approach can penalize them in terms of entrance requirements, for example, by lowering their grade point average.

Grading on a curve, however, does prepare gifted students for the effort required to compete in the real world and to realize their potential. A partial solution to this particular problem may have been found. The California university system has recently announced that special recognition will be awarded to gifted classes when calculating grade point averages for admission decisions. Grading on a curve could be used (under these conditions) with high-achieving gifted students. This approach has been effective in gifted classes that operate in school environments with low student expectations and achievements. Teachers report using this technique as a vehicle to stimulate academic growth in environments that foster mediocrity. Grading on a curve for the underachieving gifted student under most conditions, however, would be damaging. (See Clark 1983; Berk 1983; Newland 1976; and Whitmore 1980 regarding the under-achieving gifted child. See also Davis and Rimm 1985 regarding the cultural underachievement of females.)

A number of educators recommend the automatic A or B approach to grading gifted students. An automatic A or B may be approriate for highly motivated gifted children. However, gifted students, like other students, have been trained or socialized to expect grades and say they feel cheated when others receive the same grade for less work. An automatic grade can encourage students to rest on their laurels and ease through the educational system.

A few researchers have discussed alternatives to the conventional evaluation approaches. Clark (1979) suggests that the parent conference method of evaluating gifted children's progress '' is often more work, [but] many teachers feel it more clearly reflects the student's achievements and is far more diagnostic in nature.'' One of the weaknesses of this approach, as Clark (1979) suggests, is that parents are also socialized by the school system. During these conferences, many parents appear more interested in comparing their child with other competing students in his or her age bracket than in identifying their child's particular strengths and weaknesses. Syphers (1972) recommends self-diagnosis. Both of these approaches can be useful contributing elements in the evaluation process; however, neither satisfactorily stands alone, and neither would be acceptable to a school district nor match the rigor of an external assessment. In this regard, the University of California, Los Angeles, and the University of Pittsburgh lab schools are two examples of successful nongrade models, but this approach has not been widely accepted. (See Goodlad and Anderson 1959 concerning nongrading.)

No simple answer exists to the problem of grading gifted children. This brief discussion of a few recurrent problems observed during site visits helps to illuminate the pros and cons of various approaches. The problem of grading reveals the need to begin the construction of boundaries for acceptable evaluation methods and the implementation of more systematic guidelines for the wide variety of approaches currently employed in gifted programs.

Moral Character: Cheating

Cheating is a nationwide problem for students of all abilities. No evidence exists to indicate that the problem is any better or any worse in gifted and talented programs. To the extent that it is visible at all in gifted programs, cheating is a manifestation of the fact that the gifted program is a microcosm of the school and community. The GATE study documented a consistent student commitment to high ideals and social concerns throughout the state. However, real problems in the GATE program mirror those of the rest of society and warrant immediate attention. Discussing the high expectations, intense psychological pressure, and role of grades among gifted children provides a context for the problem of cheating. These pressures — when combined and uncontrolled — can have a signifi-cant impact on the moral character and development of gifted students (see Schab 1980). Extreme pressures to achieve can create an attitude that endorses achievement at all costs.

A simple test was devised for our site visits. During group interviews, the question was posed, Would you cheat if you had to? — that is, would you look at a friend's paper or the teacher's papers during an examination with the intent of copying their answer to score well on the test? The most common response was that it depended on the test. Students indicated that they would never cheat on an exam that did not significantly affect their grade. In general, they indicated that they would have to think about it and probably would cheat if it were important enough to them. I raised the stakes in our discussions and posed the following question: What if the test was the one that determined whether you would enter medical school? Typically, the overwhelming response was a qualified affirmative. Students stated they would cheat if it was only a matter of "a few questions." The discussions would typically evolve into a candid and free-flowing form and I would pose a series of the same types of questions: How would you draw the line regarding acceptable and unacceptable cheating? Could this practice lower the quality of medical students enrolled in medical schools? Do you think the practice of cheating as it has been discussed today has any implications for the quality of American health care? Most students believed they could draw the line and would not cheat if they did not think they were qualified for the position involved or if they believed it jeopardized the safety of another person. Most students believed that this type of practice, cheating on a few questions, would not lower the quality of medical students enrolled in American medical schools. There was no consensus, however, on this last question in any of the programs. The question of what they thought the implications of this type of practice were on our health care system evoked discussions that were divergent, emotional, sincere, and unending. Many students thought long-term subtle effects could shape medical practice. Some students emphasized the role of pragmatic expedience and the arbitrary quality of many examination questions and cutoff scores for acceptance into medical school programs. All gifted students interviewed took the issue seriously. They also emphasized that they did not think it would be necessary for them to cheat, but that they were prepared to cheat if it was necessary and the outcome was sufficiently important.

A majority of students interviewed throughout the state demonstrated high ideals in discussions and in their writings. Many were involved or planned to be deeply involved in some civic activity in the near future. Nevertheless, it would appear that gifted educators have neglected to deal with the issues of morality. Most students interviewed had developed a rudimentary code of situational ethics, and few had openly discussed these issues in the classroom before my visit. Gifts and talents do not preclude the need for training in social ethics and secular morality. They necessitate the need for training in moral reasoning (see Clark 1983; Sellin and Birch 1980; Tan-Willman and Gutteridge 1981; Vare 1979; and Walker 1975 regarding moral development of the gifted and talented; see also Kohlberg and Turiel 1971).

Conclusion

The most important reason for presenting these practical issues is to illustrate and sensitize program developers to the hazards that can develop from within a program. This discussion has been designed to identify specific weaknesses in gifted and talented programs throughout the state that merit immediate attention. Carefully guided introspection and self-examination can strengthen any program. Openly discussing and confronting these problems in one school may help other gifted programs throughout the country and the entire educational system deal with them. The only way to solve our educational problems is to confront them explicitly, directly, and promptly.

The most difficult and sensitive problem discussed in this chapter — ethnic mix — is a national problem. The problem threatens the survival of gifted and talented education programs. Chapter 5 confronts this issue head-on with a national test case for gifted and talented education and minority enrollment.

CHAPTER 5

A National Test Case in Peoria

This chapter presents a study of a program in Peoria, Illinois, for the gifted and talented that serves as a national test case for gifted education and minority enrollment (see Fetterman 1984b). An analysis of the program and the referral, identification, and selection mechanisms was conducted. This case study concludes that low minority enrollment need not suggest that the local school district engages in discriminatory practices or that low enrollment is explained by genetic differences between races. Instead, the study points to the impact of the community's socioeconomic characteristics on gifted enrollment. Fundamentally, the study addresses the issues of equal opportunity, ability, and achievement in American education.

Gifted programs throughout the country share the problem of low minority enrollment (see Humphreys 1984; and Lemke 1984). The Peoria school district received national attention for its failure to enroll a proportional percentage of black children in Peoria's gifted program in the early 1980s. According to *Education Week* (District's Gifted Program 1984), "The Peoria school district's gifted and talented program is in danger of losing $57,000 in state funding because of a finding [by a state study] that the program discriminates against minorities" (pp. 3–4). The minority enrollment figures did represent a red flag. Blacks represented 40 percent of the third-grade population, from which the gifted program participants were drawn. However, only 0.4 percent of this population was selected to participate in the program.

The program became a rallying point for many academics, practitioners, and politicians. The nature-nurture argument reemerged. One side argued from a Jensenist perspective (Jensen 1973, 1980; see also Reynolds and Jensen 1983), saying that low enrollment could be explained by genetic differences between races. Another group offered cultural deficit theories (see Swerdlik 1984; and Karnes 1984). Others simply called the district "racist."

73

The battle lines on the state political level were clearly drawn. The Illinois State Board of Education withheld funds because the selection process had not produced proportional minority representation in the program. The school board voted to sue the state unless the two parties could come to an agreement. In the meantime, the district refused to alter its procedures, believing that they were sound and adhered to state policies and procedures. Each party sincerely desired to resolve the matter on its own terms. A history of problems between the state and the district compounded the situation. (For a historical background of gifted and talented education in Illinois from an evaluation perspective, see Avery and Bartolini 1979; Colton 1968; Dooley et al. 1968; Herche 1979; House, Kerins, and Steele 1970, 1971a, 1971b; House et al. 1969; House, Lapan, and Kerins 1968; House, Steele, and Kerins 1970; Kerins et al. 1969; Newland 1976; Sjogren et al. 1968; Steele 1969; and Steele et al. 1970, 1971.) As a result of this standoff, the state and the district agreed that an independent evaluation of the program would be useful. The state presented a list of evaluators; however, the list included individuals who had already concluded in an earlier state study that the program selection process was seriously flawed. To complicate matters further, the assistant state superintendent said, "We will not accept any review that will not put more minorities in the program" (Hausser 1984a). The district superintendent wanted an affirmative action program rather than an academic program (see Hausser 1984a). The district wanted to know if a problem existed, but at the same time it feared a study with a foregone conclusion, for practical and political reasons. A compromise was struck. The district decided to look for an outside evaluator who had experience in gifted education and a reputation for fairness, and the state agreed to look at the report.

An evaluation of the referral, identification, and selection process was undertaken with the provision that an appraisal of the entire program would take place. If the program lacked substance or did not serve gifted children, an appraisal of its mechanisms would be an academic exercise in futility.

The Program

The Peoria Public Schools' Academically Gifted Program serves gifted children from grades four through eight. Gifted students are drawn from the entire district to study in an all-day homogeneous grouping program. Consolidating the gifted program in one building has not fostered elitist behavior. As the principal explains: "It's a leveling experience for many students who've been used to being the top student in everything they do" (Hans 1976, p. 5-A).

The gifted program began as an experimental program funded by the Allied Foundation in 1963. The district adopted the program on the basis of the evaluation results of this experiment (Bent et al. 1969). The program, which is based on a high ability and high achievement enrichment model, has a core curriculum similar to the district's curriculum. Additional activities and course requirements supplement the gifted program's basic curriculum. Special courses, including speed reading, foreign language, speech, debate, archaeology, and anthropology are also offered. Students also routinely take part in special interest activities such as intramural sports, computers, sewing, drawing, and photography.

In many respects, the enriched curriculum offers gifted students an educational experience that differs qualitatively from that offered their chronological peers in the regular school program. Speed reading is provided for seventh-grade students. According to the principal and the reading teacher, "Speed itself is *not* the primary goal." Students were observed reading at 800, 900, and 1,200 words per minute. However, they learn to vary their speed depending on the text they are reading.

Foreign language training begins in the fourth grade. The first three years of the program stress conversation. During one class, conversational contests were used to make foreign language instruction more exciting. Students were given one minute to engage in conversations using specified words. The competition required precision in comprehension and pronunciation. The program enables students to enter second- or third-year foreign language training in high school. It also provides students studying French the opportunity to live in France with a French family during the summer. In addition to reinforcing linguistic skills, this is a culturally enriching experience. One student from the 1984 class spoke enthusiastically about her experience with the rest of the class in Paris. This portion of the program, however, requires parental financial support.

Speech and debate are also part of the seventh- and eighth-grade curriculum. The speech classes require demonstrations that emphasize public speaking skills. For example, in one class a student showed how to make french fries.

Archaeological work.

Eighth-grade students also have the chance to participate in the Havana Hopewell Indians archaeological dig under the supervision of the archaeological staff of Northwestern University. They use metric measurements to record observations and findings at the site. Students plot the artifacts on graphs and sift the soil through half-inch mesh screen to catch pottery shards and other fragments. Classroom preparation for the field school is required. Courses include archaeology, anthropology, and time measurement. In one class, students measured and plotted simulated archaeological findings to prepare for the field school. Students worked in teams, cross-checking each other's work and striving for accuracy. In addition, they take an introductory research course that orients them to the scientific approach, including research concepts and techniques, and that culminates in a research paper. Students in the gifted program have made the school a successful competitor in the Junior Academy of Science State Expositions.

The Fetterman (1984b) evaluation of Peoria's gifted and talented program concluded that the district had designed a gifted education instructional program in response to the educational needs of students with both general intellectual ability and specific aptitude. In fact, the Peoria Academically Gifted Program is one of the better elementary full-day enrichment gifted programs in the country. The

Archaeological preparation.

principal provides strong educational leadership and is respected by program teachers, students, and parents. He is also viewed as a supportive individual. As one parent explained:

I think John is an asset for this school. He is very pro students and he is good for this program. And to me, what impressed me was something my daughter said. She said she was just impressed they could just talk to him just, you know, like an average person. She said, "Mom I could never do that at the other school!" I thought that was important for them to feel that they could go to John for anything. You're very apprehensive about what you do in school but if you have that fear gone, you feel you are comfortable.

The teachers in this program are dedicated and innovative educators, sensitive to the needs of gifted children. One seventh-grade student explained that these teachers "know more and they know a better way to teach it [the subject matter] so it's mostly fun and interesting." An award-winning math teacher in the program provided an insight into this student's comments: "I give . . . lots of brain-teaser kinds of problems. I'd say 50 percent of the kids will devour those and ask for more. . . . Once you get a kid to realize he has much greater potential than he ever imagined — then you've got him." Teachers design programs of instruction that address individual student differences. They often find a sharp contrast between teaching in the regular school system and in the gifted program, as one teacher remarked: "When I first started teaching [in the district] it was almost like pulling teeth. And now [in the gifted program], I'm almost running to stay in front of them" (*North Peoria Observer* 1982).

Peoria's gifted curriculum is presented in a coherent and consistent fashion. One parent who has a number of her children in the program gave her explanation for this success: "The reason I think it is a strong program is because they have clear, well-defined goals and their selection process is directly related to those goals." Organizational skills are reinforced in all classrooms. Qualities such as self-directedness and individual responsibility are encouraged, and teachers attempt to instill a sense of social concern in their students. As one teacher explained, "I would hope that I would give them some real values to use right along with their tremendous talents, so that they are of some benefit to mankind, not a detriment" (*North Peoria Observer* 1982). Students are enthusiastic and competitive learners, as well as peer educators and resources.

The school climate is conducive to the pursuit of advanced education. Like most gifted programs, this program had few discipline problems and no graffiti on the school walls. Students take pride in their school. One graduate of the program, currently a senior in college, shared his feelings in a letter to the principal:

Today I received a letter from home that included the February 17 *Journal Star* article about [the Gifted Program]. It was a fascinating piece to read — I wish I could be back at the Program. It really made me think about what sort of benefits I got from the District.

I liked being in the gifted program — regular school was boring. It's hard to forget the experiences of third grade at my [regular] home school. For example, if the class was working on homework and a student finished his work early, he was to select a book from the class library, read it, and write a book report on it. While I like reading books and didn't mind too much having to write the reports, after a while it became almost punitive to *have* to read and *have* to write just because I had worked too fast. That "enforced privilege" became an incentive to slow down and try to waste some time. There was another incident when my "Great Books" group returned to class to find ourselves placed on a panel to answer history questions thought up by other students while we were away. There's nothing wrong with a pop quiz, but being expected to show publicly how well we knew or didn't know history was both terrifying and embarrassing. That sort of situation leads to an attitude on the part of the other students (and even the teacher) of "You're so smart — so *you* tell us the answers!" That year our classes were composed of students of all ability levels, which I think was a terrible mistake. Third graders were supposed to learn the multiplication tables up to ten, but my group didn't even make it halfway through. My family had to teach them to me during the summer between third and fourth grade, when I entered the gifted program.

Entering the program was hard — a friend from [his home school] took my decision to go as a personal attack on her. At [my home school] we faced a lot of hostility on the playground from the other students. We were always "different" and "outsiders." Switching to [the Gifted Program] was great because we could finally enjoy school. The teachers were interested in us, and there was no peer pressure to slow down and be average — in fact, doing well was encouraged and respected.

I really envy the kids who go to [the program] today. They get to work with a microcomputer, learn archaeology at a real "dig," and benefit from the added experience of the teachers who have worked in the program for a while. The chance to learn a foreign language in grade school has been invaluable in more ways than one. Mastering grammatical terms and structures then has helped immensely in writing papers now. Even if my theme isn't clear, at least the form is great! I've been studying French in college, and it seems incredibly easy after German. Special programs like foreign language were both fun and rewarding.

I noticed that the class of [recent graduates] interviewed by the *Journal Star* mentioned [the Program's] freedom quite frequently as having been important to them. It was important to me, too. Being treated as a responsible person was a great privilege that I didn't appreciate until high school. I never did get used to showing hall passes to security guards or being a "number" in a PE class.

Students are encouraged to explore their own interests on the same intellectual plane. As one parent who had one child in the program and one in the regular school system elaborated:

I think the kids get more encouragement here [in the gifted program]. To achieve maybe higher than where they are. You know, I think they have the attitude that okay, the child may look and say this is difficult, but I think the teachers encourage them to try it anyway. I think they have the freedom — more freedom to do it here because of the level; they don't have to split their time between the child who may be just, you know, not so much a slow learner, but he just is not at this person's level. You're holding back and so this way I think everybody can almost work at their own level without holding back someone else. That's what I like about the program.

This facet of the program is also appreciated by students. One seventh-grade student compared the program with her old school:

[At the old school] some kids are faster and they get their work done better and some of them are slower and some couldn't do it and you had to wait for them. . . . You just had to sit there and be quiet. . . . This school is better. You switch classes — which means you have a teacher that specializes in special subjects so they can spend more time on that subject. They don't spend 15 minutes on math and you just do the assignment. You are spending a whole 45 minute period on one subject. So I understand it better.

A number of students display exceptional talent through individual efforts. For example one thirteen-year-old student's software programming accomplishments for a Silicon Valley firm have been publicized on ABC's "Good Morning, America" show. Group efforts are also common. School spirit and comraderie are evident in group classroom projects and extracurricular activities. Many of the gifted children in the program are also successful athletes in various sports.

Concern for the student's development extends outside the classroom. One parent explained how "these teachers are very supportive of sports activities," as evidenced by their routine attendence at both scrimmages and official games. One parent describes the degree of parental involvement in the support system of the program:

> Interviewer: Do you notice a difference [from the regular school system] in terms of parental involvement in the gifted program? Parent: (laughter) That's an understatement. You should have been here last night . . . [at a parent's night]. It was standing room only. There were over 300 parents. Okay, now this week at my children's other [regular] school, I will go and there will be maybe 100 parents. I mean it's definitely that much of a difference.

Parents share their appreciation of the Gifted Program with school administrators at graduation. In one letter, a parent wrote the following to the principal:

> We wish to express our appreciation of the support given to [our daughter] by you and the staff. Contrast the happy, excited, and confident teenager who completed eighth grade last week with the discouraged and despondent fifth grader who was the subject of intense peer harassment and derision three years ago and you can understand our appreciation. Your judicious actions and the staff's interested involvement undoubtedly had much to do with making [our daughter's] elementary years rewarding. She was fortunate to have the type of challenge, guidance, encouragement, and opportunity for independent development that the program provides. For all these professional benefits we are truly thankful.

Another parent's letter communicated similar sentiments:

> In a nutshell, [the Gifted Program] has let the sun shine in. My daughter always liked school, always did well, always seemed content. Now, however, school is a pure joy. The change in her is striking and only proves to me how unwittingly we ignore the needs and potential of many students because they make it so easy for us to do so. In fact, we are no doubt allowing untold numbers of youngsters to slide along at a reduced pace because we are unwilling to raise our expectations. If I could have one educational wish for Peoria youngsters, it would be that more of them could experience the sunshine that my daughter has found. Thanks for a super program.

The program's strength and community support are unquestionable. The district, however, does have areas that need innovation and improvement. Its service to gifted children between junior high school and college should be strengthened. The evaluation determined that underachieving gifted children were not served and recommended extending the program to include those students. It also recommended a mentor program and emphasized the need to collect and maintain follow-up data on graduates. Overall, however, the program was rated very highly. (This evaluation used psychometric, ethnographic, and auditing techniques. See Fetterman 1984b for the evaluation report and Fetterman 1984a and Fetterman and Pitman 1986 for details concerning ethnographic evaluation.)

The Mechanisms

Once the value of the program had been established, an analysis of the referral, identification, and selection mechanisms was warranted. The mechanisms themselves were found to be standard. On the basis of districtwide intelligence and achievement test results and teacher and principal nominations, students are referred to a neighboring university for individual intelligence testing. A selection committee screens candidates through a predetermined formula consisting of the Wechsler Intelligence Scales for Children-Revised (WISC-R) (39.65 percent), the Cognitive Abilities Test (CAT) (19.07 percent), the SRA Achievement Series (SRA) (16.09 percent), grades (15.14 percent), narrative (5.63 percent), and the Characteristics Rating Form (4.42 percent). Students are ranked according to an overall score based on this formula. The top sixty students are selected for participation in the gifted program. Periodically, students are selected to fill vacancies at various grade levels.

The evaluation found that the Peoria School District is adhering to the State Board of Education's rules, regulations, and guidelines governing the identification and selection process of gifted education reimbursement programs. Criteria for selection have been described in detail and consistently applied to children in the local educational agency population.

The district exceeds the state standards regarding the use of identification devices. The state requires a minimum of three identification devices and lists suggested methods for the district to use in identifying gifted children. The district has selected five

TABLE 1				
Districtwide Testing Cutoff Scores Based On Composite SRA and CAT Scores				
	SRA			
CAT	75-79	80-84	85-89	90-94	95-99
75-79					
80-84				X	X
85-89			X	X	X
90-94		X	X	X	X
95-99		X	X	X	X

methods from the state's list: the WISC-R (intelligence test), the SRA (achievement test), teacher recommendations, past grades (past performance), and individual rating sheets. In addition, the CAT is used. Identification criteria are established before students are selected for the program, and specific cutoff scores are adopted when standardized tests are used. A direct relationship exists between the criteria for selection and the instructional program for gifted students.

All gifted program teachers are certified and are required to meet two of the three state requirements. They must all have attended a summer training institute approved by the Office of the Superintendent of Public Instruction for teachers of the gifted, and have had at least two years (some as many as eighteen years) of experience working with gifted programs.

Refinements

Although the district met or surpassed state requirements, a review of the specific referral, identification, and selection mechanisms in practice suggested that refinements were needed. Viewing each mechanism as a gatekeeping function highlighted the significance of each problem and the nature of the necessary refinement.

For a student, referral is the first door into the gifted program. The district has three referral pools. The first is composed of third-grade students who score at the 80th percentile or above on districtwide CAT and SRA tests (see Table 1). The second pool consists of students who may have missed one of the tests by being absent, and the third pool includes individual teacher or principal nominations. Referral statistics indicated that only nine black students were referred to the 1983–84 district gifted program — four from the first pool and five from the third. Only two students were referred from five of the southern predominantly black schools in the district. One black parent explained, "I have heard from others that sometimes the teachers don't recommend the students, and it's not so much that it's because they are black, but . . . that some of the principals want to have those high achievers at their school." In other cases, the parent explained that low teacher expectations were a problem:

> The teachers walk into the school. Nothing is expected of them. They walk in and say, "All right, look at his address, where is he from? Okay, I know he is not going to be able to do this. I'm not going to spend that much time if he does not get it right away; I'm not going to spend that much time with him. Label him learning disability or slow learner. . . ." It's just so sad they feel like no one wants to teach down there. "Oh, it's boring, I can't teach those kids." They just feel they can't learn, but if they noticed, if they give these kids a little extra attention, a little encouragement, they would do well.

The number of minority students in the program can increase only if the pools of minority applicants increase. The evaluation pointed to the problem of teacher expectations and the need to conduct in-service training programs in identification and referral procedures, particularly in schools that had not referred any students to the gifted program. The evaluation recommended that teachers with the greatest predictive ability (on the basis of past performance) should help develop and conduct in-service training programs. Although it would not guarantee increased selection, such a program would be a first step toward refining the district's procedures and instruments. Increasing the pool of potentially qualified applicants is a necessary yet insufficient baseline.

Identification procedures are a second door to the program. Clark (1979) and Getzels and Dillon (1973), among others, emphasize the role of identification methods in explaining underrepresentation. The Peoria gifted and talented program had to make several modifications to answer political, pragmatic, and technical concerns. The selection committee members responsible for reviewing student tests and documents all belonged to the same school. Other schools had no representative on the committee to serve as a potential quality control and political advocate. The evaluation recommended that the district consider appointing a representative to the committee from the southern, predominantly minority schools.

A second problem involved the Characteristics Rating Form, one of the instruments to identify gifted children in the district. The form was out of date and lacked internal consistency. For example, some questions juxtaposed a "poor" rating response with a "better than a good many" rating response. An updated list of behavioral characteristics was shared with the district to enable it to modify and improve the selection process. (See Davis and Rimm 1985; Renzulli and Hartman 1971; and Tuttle and Becker 1980 for a useful collection of behavioral characteristic checklists.)

A third problem concerned the districtwide tests. The WISC-R, SRA, and CAT are acceptable and appropriate tests for a gifted program oriented toward high ability and high achievement. (See Hagen 1980 regarding the value of the WISC-R and the CAT.) A review of the district achievement test score sheets revealed no significant problem, but a minor mechanical problem did emerge. The pencil quality of recorded answers was inconsistent, which suggested that optical scoring might be affected. Such an observation seems trivial, but in a similar case the consequences were significant (Breckenridge 1984):

> Hillsborough County, Florida, public-school officials have pinpointed faulty pencils as the reason a computer misread 10,500 answer sheets for a basic-skills test taken by 85,000 students earlier this year.
>
> Administrators estimate it will cost $40,000 and take 26 days to rescore all 85,00 tests. (p. 7)

In an investigation of this type, all levels, including abstract and mechanical, must be explored. Low-graphite pencils may be used disproportionately by one segment of the population. In addition, sections of individual (SRA) score sheets were completely blank. The evaluation emphasized that this finding indicated a need for additional analysis. Further study would enable any school district to determine the frequency of the problem and any correlation with specific teachers, schools, or subpopulations.

A more substantive problem involved the CAT. One of the cutoff scores for the first pool of students (Category I referral) was based on the CAT. The lowest score was selected from the verbal, nonverbal, and quantitative elements of the test. The evaluation demonstrated how a higher measure of consistency could be achieved by selecting a single element for all students, assuming students meet an established standard on each of the CAT subtests. (The quantitative subtest appears to be the best predictor at the middle and secondary school levels.) This refinement may improve the accuracy of the match between the type of student (verbal, nonverbal, and/or quantitative ability) and the program curriculum.

As Hagen (personal communication 1985) points out, "It is extremely important that the selection process for gifted programs should be closely related to the cognitive, academic, and other demands that the program makes on students." In addition, the evaluation recommended the use of raw scores or scaled scores rather than percentiles in determining this facet of a student's eligibility for the program. Score averaging was also discussed. Hagen (personal commmunication 1985) strongly recommends that "Standard Age scores be used for selection, particularly if the selection procedure involves averaging two or more of the scores. Whenever averages of two or more of the test scores are used for selection, it is important to remember that a distribution of averages is typically less variable than the scores used to compute the average." The evaluation also noted one deviation from the conventional administration of the WISC-R: Students did not receive the vocabulary section of the test, which is the greatest predictor of achievement. Although this practice does not compromise the test validity or reliability because the four remaining subtests are averaged (see Wechsler 1974, Appendix E, p. 190), it does represent a different approach. Before the evaluation was completed, the district research director requested that the vocabulary section be administered in the future.

A more technical recommendation involved the weighting system. The following weights were given to each variable in determining the ranking score of the students: WISC-R, 39.65 percent; CAT, 19.07 percent; SRA, 16.09 percent; grades, 15.14 percent; narrative, 5.63 percent; and Characteristic Rating Form, 4.42 percent. Straight percentages, however, can give additional weight to IQ scores.

The evaluation suggested a refinement to improve the accuracy of the weighting mechanism (see Figure 1). Briefly, instead of using

Select the weights, calculate the standard deviation of the group, and divide the weight by the standard deviation. Divide this resulting figure by the smallest number resulting from this division (of weight by standard deviation). Multiply this number by 10 and round to nearest whole number. Rank students according to the score derived from this formula.

Variable Name	Weights	Standard Deviation	Weight÷ Standard Deviation	New Weight÷ Smallest Value	x10	Round
WISC-R	39.65÷3					
Verbal	13.22					
Performance	13.22					
Full-Scale	13.22					
CAT	19.07÷3					
Verbal	6.36					
Quantitative	6.36					
Nonverbal	6.36					
SRA	16.09÷3					
Composite	5.36					
Reading	5.36					
Math	5.36					
Grades	15.14					
Narrative	5.63					
Characteristics	4.42					

Figure 1
Weighting Mechanism

straight percentages for each variable, percentages could be divided by the standard deviation of the group. This refinement would further increase the accuracy of the measurement by distributing these student scores on the basis of the gifted subpopulation scores (for further details, see Guilford 1956). The evaluation also suggested that SRA raw scores could be used instead of percentiles. Adopting growth-scale values would at least represent an improvement on the use of percentiles. Raw scores can convert to normal curve equivalents (NCEs) to increase the accuracy of the measurement.

A final recommendation involved rank-ordering students eligible for a replacement slot. Periodically, students left the program, either by choice or necessity. Potential replacements, however, were not sequentially ranked according to their total scores. This practice, which was unfair to students and their parents and inconsistent with program procedures, was also a significant political liability. Politically pressured district administrators may have appreciated the latitude or discretion this loophole offered, but the small amount of discretionary power they gained was insignificant compared with the charges of preferential treatment they faced.

Overall, the evaluation concluded that district referral, identification, and selection systems were appropriate given the program's model of high ability and high achievement. Suggestions and refinements to improve the accuracy of the existing system were often geared toward enhancing the probability of increased minority representation. However, these fundamental mechanisms clearly were not the most significant cause of low minority representation in the program. The major underlying factors lay in the community, not in the school.

Socioeconomic Context of Minority Representation

The state was primarily concerned about black student representation in the district's gifted program. Black students constituted approximately 40 percent of the third grade; however, only 0.4 percent of those students participated in the gifted program. Pertinent socioeconomic data were used to explain these figures. In the district, white students constituted 60 percent of the third grade. In 1984, 55 of 737 white students (7.5 percent) were selected to participate in the gifted and talented program. Given their size in the school population, Asians were the most overrepresented group in the program, constituting 2 percent of the third-grade enrollment. However, in 1984, 3 out of 26 Asian students (12 percent) were selected to participate in the gifted program. In contrast, 2 of 475 black students (0.4 percent) were selected to participate. Clearly, blacks were statistically underrepresented in the program. Similar patterns of under- and overrepresentation resulting from social variables are common in gifted programs.

Like most communities, Peoria is not socioeconomically homogeneous. Approximately 72 percent of the black population lives in the poorer, southern section of town. The southern tracts of Peoria (essentially below the Bluff section) have by far the highest unemployment rate, the highest rate of female heads of household with children and, conversely, the lowest rate of husband-wife households. The south side has the lowest income and educational achievement levels in the community. It has also the highest percentage of renters and the highest rate of vacant commercial units. Neighborhood housing on the south side has severely deteriorated.

In contrast, the Bluff and northern sectors of Peoria are predominantly white (74 percent). These sections of the community enjoy average to very low unemployment rates and the highest rate of husband-wife households. They also have the highest incomes and educational levels in the community. The middle and northern sections of the town have the highest percentages of homeowners, few vacant commercial units, and neighborhood housing in good to excellent condition.

According to the 1980 U.S. census (U.S. Department of Commerce, issued in 1983), the median income of whites was $19,192 and that for blacks was $12,063 in Peoria. Thirty-four percent of working whites were employed in technical, sales, and administrative support occupations; 23 percent of employed blacks worked at this socioeconomic level. As one proceeded up the employment ladder, the discrepancy between blacks and whites increased. Twenty-eight percent of employed whites had jobs in managerial and professional specialty occupations — 16 percent in the professional category. In contrast, only 13 percent of employed blacks worked in this economic group — 9 percent in professional fields. Similarly, 29.5 percent of the black population lived below the poverty line, compared with 5.6 percent of the white population.

Gifted enrollment statistics are a product of societal forces outside the classroom. These socioeconomic variables strongly influence this gifted program's enrollment statistics (see Barbe 1956 regarding socioeconomic variables). Given such differences in Peoria, disproportional representation in a program geared toward high ability and high achievement is not suprising. A great number of social forces inhibit proper academic preparation of blacks in Peoria, ranging from low incomes to insufficient educational background. Conversely, white families in Peoria have the advantages of higher incomes and better educational backgrounds than blacks.

The evaluation had to take these variables into account when evaluating program enrollment statistics. Looking simply at IQ scores leads to invidious comparisons between blacks and whites. In an ideal world in which all students share the advantages of a supportive, enriched background, IQ scores would have more meaning and proportional representation could be expected. Peoria's vast socioeconomic differences, however, make such expectations unrealistic.

Interpreting the meaning of enrollment data also requires the evaluator to make appropriate comparisons with other communities. For example, comparing Evanston's (Illinois) gifted program enrollment with Peoria's program enrollment would be comparing apples and oranges. Evanston is a more socioeconomically homogeneous community than Peoria; it has only a $4,000 difference between the median income of whites and blacks. Similarly, 33 percent of employed whites work in technical, sales, and administrative support positions, and 34 percent of employed blacks hold jobs within this same occupational group. Educational differences are not as great as those between blacks and whites in Peoria. In addition, fewer families live below the poverty line, and the ratio between blacks and whites below the poverty line is much smaller than the ratio in Peoria. A significant difference exists between Peoria's and Evanston's gifted programs as well. Evanston's model includes a visual and performing talents category. These socioeconomic and program model differences produce markedly different sets of enrollment figures. Thus, delineating pertinent variables in the process of making program comparisons is essential to an accurate appraisal.

In sum, socioeconomic variables must be considered in meaningfully interpreting the significance of a gifted program's enrollment data. In Peoria's case, the socioeconomic context provides much of the basis for its 40 percent/.04 percent minority selection ratio.

Quota Systems and Equality of Results

Problems of unequal representation are often addressed by imposing a quota, making proportional enrollment a legislative process. In Peoria, the district faces State Board of Education pressures to establish greater minority representation in its gifted program. A quota system in Peoria would produce proportional representation and be politically expedient. However, a simple percentage quota system — unrelated to existing criteria — would have significant and potentially deleterious effects on the program and on district enrollment.

Peoria's program is designed for high-ability and high-achieving students. This model serves motivated, goal- and achievement-oriented students with high intellectual potential. Funds limit the program to sixty students. Such fiscal contraints already cause a loss of district enrollment; many eligible students (not included in the sixty selected) are lost to private schools.

A simple percentage quota system in this district would mean abandoning existing program standards and selection criteria. The program curriculum would have to be revamped for high achievers rather than for gifted children. In addition, a quota would jeopardize the concept of fair selection. Districtwide enrollment attrition is another probable outcome of this approach, since quota systems reduce program slots through preassignment. High-scoring nonminority students, excluded from the program by the quota system, would probably leave the district enrollment rosters as well.

The larger mission of the gifted program is also at issue. Peoria's program is, by its nature, designed to meet the needs of children at the margins of intellectual distribution. Implementing a quota system redefines the term *gifted* and equates equal opportunity with equal ability — an egalitarian fallacy. Applying a simple percentage quota system, unrelated to existing selection criteria, to a gifted program makes no more sense than applying such a system to an athletic team. The program's purpose is to select and serve children with specific intellectual and motivational needs and qualities. Students having the highest predicted criteria performance should be selected. These criteria for program selection should be based on statistical measures supplemented by more subjective measures.

At the same time, scores must be viewed realistically. The difference between an IQ score of 130 and one of 128 is academic. The child who scores 128 will, in all probability, perform as well as the student who scores 130. Comparing scores is much like comparing stereo specifications. The difference between a receiver that has a range of 20 to 20,000 MHz and a receiver that has a range of 17 to 25,000 MHz is extremely small, given that the human ear can only hear between 20 and 20,000 MHz. Similarly, a quota system that selects for minority status within an acceptably high ability and achievement range need not require perfect numerical comparability with competing students. Such an approach would not undermine the program.

The faulty equation of equal opportunity with equal ability is followed by an equally misleading equation — that of equal opportunity with equal achievement or results.

One intellectually important consequence of the Coleman
enquiry into educational inequalities was that concepts of equality
began to polarize around two dominant principles: one was the
old traditional value of equality of opportunity, but the other
was the newly appreciated — if not newly conceived — idea
of equality of results . . . as Coleman clearly preceived, when
equal results were achieved in academic records it did not follow
as a matter of course that they sprang from equality of
conditions in the schools. Beyond this difficulty, the somewhat
crude results thrown up by test scores and other school records
could too easily be transmuted from methods of measurement
into educational aims. When the aim of the schools was to
achieve an equality of recorded measurement the system might
be in working order, but some doubt would arise as to whether
it was a system of education. Educational specialists would find
nothing to surprise them in this problem. Its most acute form
had long afflicted America's more gifted children, frequently
held back from anything like their full potentialities by the
stubborn pace of satisfied mediocrity. When quality meant equal
opportunity for each child to develop fully his or her own
potential, it could not be easily reconciled with the view of
equality which aimed to produce a steady stream of similar
products and failed to offer the incentive, the equipment, or
the intelligence needed by children of innately superior abilities
(Pole 1978, p. 352).

The issues of equal opportunity, ability, and achievement or results
can have a profound effect on the operation of gifted education
programs. These basic philosophical concerns, as well as pragmatic
and political concerns, must be addressed before any alteration of
a program's existing model is undertaken.

Conclusion

The evaluation's findings were presented to the school board in
a controversial and highly publicized atmosphere, reflecting the
political tensions that ran though the entire study. Three television
channels and a handful of newpaper and radio reporters covered the
affair. Cameras were rolling; floodlights and microphones were
everywhere. The board heard a point-by-point report and then

explored specific points in greater detail and asked for additional suggestions. At the subsequent press conference, some reporters pressed for a vindication of the city. Others viewed this occasion as an opportunity to strengthen the state's case.

Predictably, television coverage presented as many interpretations of the evaluation report as there were reporters. One anchorman reported that the Stanford researcher had given the program a "gold seal." Another anchorwoman reported "mixed findings" by the Stanford professor. A third reporter emphasized the socioeconomic factors discussed in the report. *Education Daily* emphasized the evaluation recommendations regarding "refining the weighting system for tests to select students" and the warning that "teachers too often have low expectations of black children" (see Hausser 1984b, p. 8).

For its part, the district considered each finding and recommendation on its own merits. The district made more than twenty-three program changes based on the evaluation recommendations.

> Some of the changes include having a representative from the Valley schools, which have a higher percentage of blacks, on the selection committee for the program; training teachers in Valley schools where few or no students have been referred to the program to recognize gifted students; establishing quality controls on the system used to select students; and developing a more definitive process for ranking students for selection. (Hausser 1984a, p. C-6)

The board president sent a copy of the report and program changes to the state superintendent of education to resolve Peoria's ongoing conflict. The district agreed to increase the pool of minority applicants. However, the director of research recognized that "increasing the pool of minority students in the referral group will not necessarily increase the number of minorities selected as long as the program is maintained at its original intent and present purpose" (Griffith 1984a, p. 12).

According to the district's research director, "Our interest is to have an academically gifted program for children with high ability who have proven academic achievement" (Griffith 1984b, p. D-4). Each community selects the type of program it believes to be most advantageous for its children. As Whitmore (1980) points out, "Methods of identification are determined by the goals of the program for which students are being selected" (p. 19). Peoria's model is highly selective and is only one of many excellent gifted and talented program models.

Some programs have broken Peoria's criteria into separate parts for selection consideration: high achievement for one group and high ability for another. Using the high-achievement category alone and lowering IQ standards for economically disenfranchised students has been successful in increasing minority enrollment in San Diego. However, a different kind of program is needed to accommodate students selected under these arrangements. Moreover, some difficulties with retention have arisen with this selection system. A program that places greater emphasis on talents and creativity than on academic giftedness would probably increase minority represen-tation. Such a focus would, however, require redesigning the pro-gram structure and curriculum as well as staff configuration.

These options were presented to the district to enable it to make a more informed decision. The district chose to select for students with high ability and high achievement and decided to retain its criteria in the future. The state superintendent of education offered to sit down with district officials to avoid a lawsuit. ''We don't shrink from lawsuits, but we think there are better ways to settle things'' (School Officials 1984, p. A-5). The district, however, was forced to take the case to court and won.

The Peoria program was a test case for a basic problem in gifted education programs throughout the country. The evaluation of Peoria's program demonstrated that problems in the classroom often spring from the local community (see also Tannenbaum 1983, p. 353). Program and community variables must be thoroughly evaluated before conclusions about a district's predisposition or a subpopula-tion's ability are made. Since schools often reflect societal forces, inequities in the community will create inequities in its schools. To accuse the schools and school programs of being the sole cause of such problems is an example of blaming the victim.

Chapter 6 expands our scope from the national to the interna-tional level. The next chapter builds on the discussion of excellence and equity. Instead of viewing the problem from a national perspec-tive, however, and focusing on competing groups within a culture, it focuses on the gifted cross-culturally. This exploration captures the essence of many nations' ambivalence, as they attempt to balance an egalitarian ethic with the special needs of gifted individuals.

CHAPTER 6

An International Overview

Many kinds of gifted programs exist throughout the world, each reflecting its unique cultural and ideological context. The desire to meet the needs of gifted children is the common thread that ties them together.

Ambivalence toward the gifted is a cross-cultural phenomenon. Almost every nation recognizes the value of the gifted as scientists, artists, or social and political leaders, yet this recognition is juxtaposed against ignorance. Lack of understanding of the full meaning of equal educational opportunity compromises the validity of this concept. Too often, a well-intentioned, strong egalitarian ethic overshadows the special needs of the gifted, who require special attention much as disabled persons or athletes require special educational attention to fulfill their potential. An egalitarian ethic often confuses equality of opportunity with equality of ability, a philosophical position that obscures individual educational needs.

However, nations that hold this position have also faced the reality of intracultural diversity — individual differences — and have had to accommodate such differences in practice. Policies, programs, identification criteria, and curricula for the gifted and talented may vary in quality, consistency, or explicitness, but they exist in almost every nation. This chapter presents a variety of approaches to meet the needs of the gifted internationally. In some countries, such as the Soviet Union, ideology is circumvented by special programs and an elaborate network of after-school programs. In other countries, the egalitarian ethic and special programs for the gifted coexist in a contradictory but constructive atmosphere. Evaluation assessments of these programs have been included whenever appropriate material was available.

The Soviet Union

Historical Background

The educational traditions of the Soviet Union are filled with contradictions. One tradition, which traces to Leo Tolstoy's school at Yasnaya Poliana, was to espouse complete freedom of expression for the child. In Tolstoy's school, the teacher served as facilitator and resource, "stripped of all disciplinary powers over his pupils" (Hans 1962, p. 99). In contrast, the tzarist government emphasized conformity and indoctrination. Nationalism and adherence to the Orthodox faith were central objectives of its educational mission. Prerevolutionary education consisted of a multitrack *Gymnasium* system for the upper 7 percent of the school population. This system was designed to reinforce the existing class structure.

During the revolution, in 1917, radical reforms were initiated and the tzar's control over education was abolished. Mass education replaced the multitrack system. Commissar of Education Lunacharsky emphasized humanistic views (Dunstan 1978, p. 17), and the new Soviet education policy stressed the development of individual aptitude. *The Basic Principles of the Unified Labour School* (1918) stated the following:

> We do not forget the right of an individual to his own peculiar development. It is not necessary for us to cut short a personality, to cheat it, to cast it into iron moulds, because the stability of the socialist community is based not on the uniformity of a barracks, not on artificial drills, not on religious and aesthetic deceptions, but on actual solidarity of interests.

Disciplinary control, homework, and examinations were eliminated. At the age of thirteen, children were allowed to manage their own programs. This approach was soon found unwieldy and impractical, and the pendulum swung back toward control. The Education Act of 1923 directed that all education serve the proletarian class in a direct and practical fashion.

A.S. Bubnov replaced Lunacharsky, and vocationalism was the order of the day. The decree "On the Primary and Secondary School" reinstated a traditional instructional format. Intelligence testing greatly facilitated identification of the intellectually gifted. However, such testing and special grouping fell into disfavor in the 1930s.

Historical materialism rests on a doctrine of equal ability. Pavlovian psychologists argue that all children are equally capable of learning; consequently, giftedness is not considered an innate or even partially innate characteristic. Yet, intelligence test results suggested genetic differences in Soviet society. To disprove this finding, Soviet psychologists concluded that tests adopted from the West were better measures of environmental influence than of innate ability. In addition, Soviet educators argued that special grouping would foster anticollectivist and elitist behavior. In 1934, ability grouping and intelligence testing were condemned because they proved "special giftedness and special right to life of the exploiting classes and of 'superior races' while on the other hand [rationalizing] the physical and spiritual doom of the working classes and 'inferior races' " (see "Narodnoe obrazovanie vs SSSR," as cited in Roeper 1960, p. 362). In 1936, intelligence testing was banned in the Soviet Union. The 1936 decree, "On Pedagogical Perversions in the System of the Narkomprosy," ended any plans for a differentiated education for the gifted (Dunstan 1978, p. 24). Students were placed in a lock-step program, used identical textbooks, and progressed through the system according to an a priori timetable.

In 1960, the Academy of Pedagogical Sciences published the *New System of Popular Education in U.S.S.R.* This collection of articles and memoranda refocused Soviet education in an effort to reconcile these contradictory traditions. The new educational system was designed to produce a "harmonious combination of individual and social interests . . . [and to] assure general culture and the development of all the abilities and talents of the rising generation." Khrushchev (1958) advocated schools for gifted children and emphasized the role of gifted children in this new system. However, he received little support from the Central Committee of the Communist Party.

The instrumental role of *odarennye deti* (gifted children) in science — particularly in space technology — sparked a surge of interest in gifted education. Today, special schools for academically talented children have official sanction in the Soviet Union. In addition, separate schools for children gifted in the fine arts continue to receive generous government support.

Kozyr' (personal communication 1985), Chief of the International Relations Department in the Academy of Pedagogical Sciences, provides a picture of the administrative structure and mission of art schools for the gifted child in the USSR. In the process of painting this picture, Kozyr' provides an insight into the nature of the Soviet Union's approach to all gifted children.

> The art schools for children, which are under the authority of the Ministry of Culture of the USSR and RSFSR, originate in the system of mass education with children in general education schools. The strictly "gifted" child, as should be supposed, enters in the so-called "middle level art schools," which work at the higher scholarly art institutions in Moscow and Leningrad, and in the capitals of the union republics. Basically, these schools replenish the cadres of professional artists and are under the jurisdiction of the Academy of Arts of the USSR, which develops and authorizes the programs for them.

The pressing issue of how to balance a commitment to nourishing the talents of the gifted with a desire to socialize children to function as equals is as much a problem in the USSR as it is in the United States. Kozyr' (personal communication 1985) clearly communicates the USSR's antielitist position in his description of the *Young Artist* journal: "This journal, to some extent, reflects the existing approach in the USSR to the work with the gifted children: its mass character, accessibility, widespread propaganda [or promotion] of arts and lack of orientation toward the 'chosen ones.' " Such a contradictory position may place great stress on children in this environment; however, it parallels gifted children's experience throughout the world.

Gifted Education in the Soviet Union Today: Young Pioneer Palaces and Circles

Ideologically, the Soviet Union, like the United States, displays an ambivalent attitude about intellectually gifted children. Both countries attempt to balance the demands of the group with the needs of individual freedom. Both the United States and the USSR ideologically oppose the concept of a privileged class. Both countries fear that segregating the intellectually gifted will create such a class, and yet they permit special segregated training for gifted students in the fine arts. At the same time, both superpowers recognize the value and special needs of the intellectually gifted child and have devised a variety of approaches — including homogeneous grouping — to serve those needs. The Soviet Union's answer to this dilemma includes experiments with mathematics and physics boarding schools, special schools, optional studies, and in-class enrichment programs (see Dunstan 1978, pp. 116–150, 151–176, 176–196, and 197-208). Their traditional approach to the gifted centers is intense enrichment activities after the school day.

Soviet education provides an impressive extracurricular system for all children — the Young Pioneer Palaces (see Kreusler 1976, pp. 159–163; Dunstan 1978, pp. 209–217; and O'Dell 1983, pp. 117–120). Palaces are located throughout the Soviet Union. They use mass education to instill national pride and patriotism, including indoctrination into communist ideology. According to Kreusler (1976), "The purpose of the youth organizations is to educate a new type of man, a loyal citizen unquestioningly carrying out the orders of the Party, one who is selfless and devoted to the cause of communism" (p. 158). The Young Pioneer Organization is designed to educate "all children in a collectivist spirit and to prepare them to live in a communist society" (Kreusler 1976, p. 159). Ideology aside, this system is suited perfectly to the needs of the gifted child. The Young Pioneer Palace system consists of more than forty-five hundred houses and palaces for children aged five to seventeen. These palaces are designed to enable children to pursue their specialized interests and hobbies in supervised amateur circles. The houses provide up-to-date laboratories, art studios, equipment, and instruction. They offer the gifted child opportunities to go beyond the classroom curriculum and to explore topics of interest in depth. They have fostered a number of special student projects. A tenth-grade electronics club operated a closed circuit television station. The Natural Science Lovers developed a valuable hybrid melon. Children conduct scientific work and report on the results of their research at scientific meetings. Professional mentors guide these students. Local and national competition helps to identify gifted children. Thus the purpose of these clubs and circles is to identify and shape specially talented students for future roles in adult Soviet society.

The largest and most famous palace is the Moscow City Young Pioneer Palace (*Children's Palace* 1984). Over fifteen thousand children attend this facility twice a week. The palace has more than nine hundred circles and clubs, ranging from the Cosmonauts' Club to the Physical Training Group. Laboratories and workshops are provided for the children's instruction. The government subsidizes this palace at a cost of 2.5 million rubles each year.

Technical Circles. Science and technology circles are popular in the Moscow palace. Approximately eighteen hundred children participate in these circles, designing and building model sports cars and radio and television sets. Building model aircraft, ships, go-carts, and rockets is also popular. Children enter their models in local, national, and international competitions. Many of the childrens' inventions are commissioned by the government, including miniature tractors and drilling rigs. A railway modeling group plans to build working models of locomotives with the assistance of the Kiev Railway Station.

The Young Astronomers' and Cosmonauts' Clubs are equipped with an observatory and planetarium. More than seven hundred children attend the Astronomers' Club. The younger students are taught how to make rotary celestial maps, sundials, and angle gauges. Students in the sixth and seventh grades study theoretical astronomy and build telescopes and other equipment. They also present papers in their circles based on independent astronomical investigation and observation. The staff of such institutions as the Institute of Space Studies, the Sternberg Astronomy Institute, the Nuclear Physics Institute, and the USSR Astronomical and Geodesic Society guide students in these circles. They suggest topics of investigation in conjunction with their own research interests, and they monitor the students' progress. Students often report their findings to the appropriate academy. This program is functionally equivalent to a sophisticated mentor approach in U.S. gifted and talented education.

The Cosmonauts' Club is organized much like the Astronomers' Club. It has approximately two hundred members. They learn about spacecraft design, and several students have won prizes in international competitions. The students also conduct medicobiological experiments for cosmonauts under the guidance of appropriate professors. Former club members have entered research institutions and related pragmatic professions.

Naturalists' Circles. The Moscow palace has fifty-nine naturalists' circles, and approximately nine hundred children belong to these circles. Members attend field trips to the forest and zoo to enhance their zoological or botanical knowledge. The circles are divided into four basic categories: aquarium fish breeding, cactus growth, nature conservation, and zoology. Students conduct independent research projects under the supervision of various organizations, including the Institute of Chemical Physics, the Institute of Organic Chemistry, the Lenin Pedagogical Institute, the Central Botanical Gardens, and the Moscow Zoo. Members of these clubs present the results of their findings to their peers in the circles and at scientific conferences.

International Friendship Club. The Friendship Club is designed to provide students with civic and political education. The club is composed of fifty-five circles. Representatives of each circle meet once a week at the club's board meeting. The club emphasizes the role of Marxian solidarity throughout the world, and members are encouraged to become politically active. Activities may range from antinuclear war demonstrations to sending toys to Nicaraguan children. In addition, students interested in learning about different cultures join this club. Younger students learn such languages as English and German, and older students may learn to speak Japanese, Norwegian, Danish, Greek, or Bulgarian. The club often has journalists as invited speakers and holds discussions of international events. Members of the club correspond with students in seventy-six countries.

Song and Dance Ensemble. The song and dance ensemble entertains television and concert hall audiences. Members also perform internationally. Approximately fifteen hundred students belong to the ensemble, ranging in age from six to seventeen. The ensemble is not open to all children — talented children must pass three levels of competition. Soviet composers such as Shostakovich and Molchanov have written works for these children to perform. Famous mezzo-sopranos and Bolshoi ballet stars began their training in this ensemble. This club also has a drama group, the Young Moscovites Theatre, and a film studio. Students learn the art of script writing, direction, and cinematography. The Seven Colours of the Rainbow club instructs young painters; successful painters present lectures. Students give exhibitions of their work and enter contests. Approximately nine hundred children attend classes in painting, sculpture, graphic arts, and a variety of other fine arts, including the folk arts.

Sports Center. The Moscow palace also provides sports training for children. Swimming, hiking, camping, gymnastics, football, skiing, figure skating, and chess are offered. More than fifteen hundred members specialize in particular sporting activities. Coaches screen members to determine their interests and suitability, and skilled coaches supervise their training. Some Olympic champions have trained at this center, and most sports activities are directed toward competitions. World class chess champions have also emerged from the center.

Other Schools and Programs. Many other schools and programs exist for the academically gifted child and the talented child in the fine arts. Moscow State University successfully identified mathematically gifted children using a Mathematics Olympiad (Roeper 1960, p. 373). The Ministry of Education authorized a special class for mathematically precocious ninth-grade students (Vogeli 1968). Special boarding schools for students with an exceptional mathematical aptitude were established in 1963, including the Moscow School of Mathematics and Physics and the Novosibirsk School of Mathematics and Physics. Olympiads in mathematics, physics, and literature and contests in biology, geography, and philology help to identify gifted children throughout the country (see Berezina and Foteyeva 1972; Glowka 1970; and Dunstan 1978).

Full- and part-time music schools include the Central Musical School, which is designed to produce professional performers, and the Gnessin Music Pedagogical Institute, which trains music educators. The Moscow Ballet School, the Vaganova School in St. Petersburg, and the Leningrad Ballet School are highly selective centers, providing intensive, all-day, year-round training. The Moscow Art School is a nationally competitive institution. Students participate in international exhibitions (see Roeper 1960 for more information about these programs).

According to Brickman (1979), these programs represent adaptations to the reality of intellectual differences: "It is clear that the special school for the gifted, whether artistically or academically, has won a place in the Soviet school system. The collective society becomes flexible enough to make some more equal than others" (p. 322). Soviet society, like American society, has learned to accommodate both the needs of certain individuals and those of the larger society. The decision to serve the gifted in the Soviet Union is of less interest than the method selected to meet their needs. After-school programs, in particular, are more elaborate than any existing system and are thus worthy of consideration and emulation.

Australia

Like the Soviet Union, Australia demonstrates an ambivalent attitude toward the gifted. However, it has also developed a programmatic response to the needs of the gifted.

The Australian Department of Education and Youth Affairs provides a useful insight into the role of gifted children. "The tendency in most states is to treat gifted children as valuable members of the normal school society and to educate them in comprehensive schools which may provide special enrichment programs in addition to normal school work" (1984, p. 22). Most states evidence a strong egalitarian ethic and are wary of special grouping for gifted children. In fact, an "anti-intellectual core [exists] in most state and non-state departments" (Braggett 1984, p. 71). This attitude places both the gifted child and the teacher at a severe disadvantage. The child does not receive the special attention he or she requires, and the teacher is frustrated by a lack of experience or expertise with the gifted child in the normal classroom environment (see Lett 1976).

This dilemma characterizes the overall cultural background of gifted education in Australia. However, Australia is not a homogeneous entity. A continuum exists from supportive to obstructive attitudes about gifted education. A variety of associations for gifted and talented children in most states serve to organize parents, educators, and administrators. In addition, a wide variety of programs have been developed to meet the needs of the gifted in each state. Australian programs for the gifted include enrichment activities, school clusters or consortia, special interest centers, gifted classes and schools, and acceleration.

Western Australia is one of the states that support gifted education. In any society, official policy statements, when accompanied by appropriate funding, set the tone for education programs. Western Australia was the first state to publish an official policy statement for the gifted (Western Australia 1978). Its policy encourages student testing for selection and placement in primary and secondary schools. Victoria is the only state that has not issued a policy statement about the gifted. South Australia's policy has a strongly egalitarian tone and is directed toward "fostering gifts and talents in children" (South Australia 1983). South Australia does not differentiate between the gifted child and the normal child; instead, its educational policy focuses on the gifts of all children.

Enrichment

States that consider full-day classes or gifted schools inappropriate or elitist generally adopt enrichment activities. New South Wales (1983), Tasmania (1984), Queensland (1983), and Australian Capital Territory (1983) have each adopted enrichment approaches. Braggett (1984) identifies four generic enrichment approaches in use throughout Australia: extracurricular activities, minicourses, extension activities, and independent study. Extracurricular activities include camping, photography, stamp collecting, and painting. Minicourses include studies of pollution, drama, archaeology, human behavior, and family stress. Extension activities involve additional instruction about topics in a course of particular interest to the student or teacher. Independent study projects allow students to pursue topics of interest in depth with appropriate supervision.

School Clusters or Consortia

Cooperative arrangements between schools enable states to pool their resources and to provide special courses and programs for the gifted. In Tasmania, five schools coordinate efforts to provide gifted courses. In Adelaide, thirteen secondary schools work together to provide a differentiated curriculum. The Gifted Children Task Force in Victoria has organized twenty-four school clusters that provide over four hundred course units for the gifted. Each school devises its own identification and selection procedures.

Special Interest Centers

Western Australia supports twenty-two elementary Special Interest Centers that serve both metropolitan and rural regions. Students attend the center for half a day each week for two years during their fourth and fifth grades. Students scoring in the top 3 percent on verbal and nonverbal tests are eligible for admission to Special Interest Centers. Socioeconomic level, geographic location, and other factors are also taken into consideration in determining eligibility for participation. Special programs are also provided for gifted aboriginal children. These culturally sensitive programs have significantly improved attendance by aboriginal students.

Secondary Special Interest Centers are schools within schools. Teachers with expertise in the areas of music, art, and language provide a specialized program for gifted children within the regular high school. This instruction supplements the required high school curriculum. In 1967, Western Australia — and South Australia in 1976 — were the first states to offer programs for the gifted. Western Australia conducts talent searches to identify gifted students for special art classes, language schools, dance and theater arts classes, and special music schools. Student portfolios are presented for evaluation as part of the selection process. Once selected, students must complete normal school requirements and in addition receive instruction from artists after school hours and during the weekends.

Four Special Interest Music Centers exist in Adelaide. Musically talented students receive specialized instruction thoughout their high school training. Fremont High School is a well-known Special Interest Music Center in Adelaide. Instructors provide students specialized musical training, including music theory, music history, and composition. Students also receive training in a wide variety of concert instruments. In addition, they are encouraged to experiment with integrating the arts, combining music with visual and performing arts and creative writing.

Special Classes and Schools

Special classes for the gifted are called "opportunity classes." In 1932, New South Wales began offering opportunity classes for fifth- and sixth-grade students for two years. Intelligence scores are part of the eligibility criteria. The classes are designed to provide enrichment opportunities for gifted students. Since such classes are not always politically marketable in New South Wales, the Department of Education does not plan to expand its existing system (Services for Children 1983, p. 6).

Western Australia offers thirteen full-time extension classes for grades six and seven. Students who enroll in these classes must complete the standard school curriculum and in addition must pursue such areas as music, drama, human biology, German, and ethics. Teaching approaches range from lectures to self-paced learning centers.

Western Australia also offers special classes in nine urban secondary schools. In addition to addressing the needs of gifted children, these classes inhibit the gifted migration to private schools. Students are grouped together for instruction in core subjects for two to three years. Core courses focus on the development of abstract thinking, cultural edification, building self-confidence, and leadership skills (Kelmscott 1983). Students must also take electives in the regular school program during this period.

Students from across the state apply for admission to these classes. Verbal and nonverbal intelligence tests identify gifted students. In addition, special provisions have been developed to identify culturally different children. These programs have served as models for the regular school programs, suggesting alternative teaching and learning patterns and encouraging "high standards of excellence" (Academic Extension Branch 1984).

Acceleration

Australian education is "characterized by a lock-step method of progression whereby children are promoted by age rather than ability" (Braggett 1984, p. 65). Acceleration is therefore a politically sensitive approach to serving gifted children. Nevertheless, grade skipping is a practice adopted by every state. Students may be accelerated through one or more grades as a result of the combined pressures of students, parents, teachers, and administrators. But such acceleration is rarely the result of a detailed, long-range plan — more often it is the most rapid way to relieve administrative pressure and to solve a serious educational structural deficiency.

Students also accelerate in stages; that is, they may advance in mathematics and remain in their regular classes until they are ready to make a complete shift to the next level. This approach is often used as a transitional approach to full acceleration in all subjects. Students are also allowed to complete the normal curriculum at an accelerated pace using a multiple-levels accelerated approach. In 1981, nine Secondary Special Placement Schools in Western Australia developed individualized acceleration programs for gifted students, including Applecross (1983), Duncraig (1983), Kelmscott (1983), and Swanbourne (1984) senior high schools. These programs allow students to progress at their own pace in specific subjects at various grade levels simultaneously. For example a student is able to pursue eleventh- and twelfth-grade courses in some subjects while completing tenth-grade courses in others during the same year.

The University High School in Melbourne offers gifted students the opportunity to complete their studies at an accelerated pace without completing the normal curriculum. Students enter a curriculum differentiated from the mainstream curriculum which enables them to complete their studies in two-thirds the normal time required to graduate. They are also allowed to take university courses on a part-time basis as part of their program. The sophistication of the specific program selected in Australia, like in most countries, is a function of the communities' commitment to the gifted.

New Zealand

New Zealand's educational policies are shaped by a strongly egalitarian ethic, even though New Zealand officially recognizes the need to alter core curricula to meet the needs of gifted children (Department of Education 1984, p. 25). Parkyn's work (1948, 1953, 1963, 1976, and 1984) has been exemplary in sensitizing New Zealand policymakers and educators to the needs of the gifted and their role in society. In addition, his work has expanded the gifted community's perception of giftedness from the rational and scientific through the aesthetic to the ethical dimension. Successful local efforts work to develop gifted programs in New Zealand (see McAlpine and McGrath 1972; and McAlpine 1984). The Christchurch Association for Gifted Children of New Zealand provides coordination and leadership in the area of gifted education. The association also plays a useful role in shaping New Zealand's educational policy. However, New Zealand lacks a strong or systematic commitment to gifted education (see Winterbourn 1962; and Hill 1976). The New Zealand Department of Education report clearly states that "too early specialization, either by way of vocational training or the narrow pursuit of specialized academic interest, [is] undesirable" (Department of Education 1984, p. 9). Overall, Reid's (1984) depiction of New Zealand's approach to gifted education is the most accurate available. He says that the system is "very variable in terms of providing an appropriately differentiated education for the gifted and talented," and continues, "We appear to lack a real long-term commitment by both professional educators and administrators" (p. 179). In comparison with Australia, New Zealand is much less generous toward the gifted. In fact, New Zealand has one of the weakest commitments to the gifted in this cross-cultural comparison.

Federal Republic of Germany

West Germany's gifted programs are still in their infancy. This situation is in part a result of the country's factionalism and of its historical development. West Germany is divided into ten states, and a separate ministry of education exists for each state. Therefore, there is no such thing as a Federal Ministry of Education'' (Koelle 1962, p. 259). Traditionally, students have been tracked for either work or higher education. Exceptions have been made for the gifted, for example, by the Mannheim School System (1895–1923), which provided special classes for academically talented students. In addition, competency examinations for higher education were offered for individuals who lacked a formal secondary education. These exams included *Begabtenprugung* in 1923, *Prufung für die Zulassung zum Hochschulstudium ohne Reifezeugnis* in 1952, and *Zweiter Bildungsweg* in the 1950s. The Deutsches Institut für Talentstudien (German Institute for Talent Studies) also served the gifted individual in the work force. The Institute was designed ''to establish a far-reaching scheme of help to individual workers, farmers, and other employees with the purpose of offering a stimulus for further education and life-long learning'' (Schairer 1962, p. 274). The *Bund-Lander-Kommission für Bildungsplanung* (Federal-State Commission for Educational Planning) has recommended that states make provisions for the identification of gifted children in primary school. Pupils who excel in a specific topic are allowed to study together. This approach is referred to as *Kernunterricht*. In addition, the *Gymnasium* offers specialized instruction in language, mathematics, music, agriculture, and science (see Schultze and Fuhr 1968, 1973). However, the approach to identification, selection, and treatment of gifted children has been rudimentary.

West Germany's program for the gifted is an artifact of its existing educational system. Students are progressively screened throughout their educational training from *Grundschule* (elementary school), through *Hauptschule* (a fifth- to ninth-year secondary school with links to vocational education) and *Realschule* (a demanding fifth- to tenth-year secondary school that prepares students for nonprofessional careers), to the *Gymnasium* (a fifth- to thirteenth-year secondary school that prepares students for institutions of higher education). (See *The Educational System in the Federal Republic of Germany* 1982 for additional details about the German educational system.) In the *Gymnasium*, ''each year promotion into the higher form is granted or withheld by the teachers' conference on the merits of the pupil's achievement'' (Koelle 1962, p. 263). Standardized intelligence tests are rarely used. Evaluation typically depends on written papers, grades, and recommendations. Moreover, according to Hoogh (in press), "the promotion of the gifted currently takes the form almost exclusively of programmes on special topics. . . .the vast majority of such programmes are offered as extracurricular activities."

This pattern is currently changing. Many exciting developments are taking place in Germany today that are directed toward a more systematic focus on the gifted child. For example, Hoogh (in press) is experimenting with an individual model approach, emphasizing home study accompanied by advice and consultation in the school. In addition, the University of Hamburg is conducting a systematic search for mathematically talented twelve-year-old children, modeled after the Study of Mathematically Precocious Youth (SMPY) (Stanley and Benbow 1982), and offers a long-term weekend enrichment program to the highest-scoring children (Wagner and Zimmermann, in press). The *Bundesministerium für Bildung und Wissenschaft* in Bonn is funding a half-million-mark project, the Identification and Guidance of Highly Gifted Children, to study identification criteria for the gifted. The study is a six-year longitudinal project. "The aims of the planned study are: (1) the development of a suitable diagnostic instrument for means of identification, (2) the development and testing of concepts and models for guidance and counseling of gifted children (including consultation of parents and teachers), and (3) the observation of the development of the gifted in a longitudinal study" (Heller 1985, p. 7). Professor Kurt Heller of the Universitat München toured the United States during the summer of 1984 to solicit opinions and information about this project. He met with Professors Feldhusen at Purdue; Stanley at Johns Hopkins; Hagen, Passow, and Tannenbaum at Columbia; Cronbach, Fetterman, and Haertel at Stanford; Nash at Texas A&M; and Torrance at Georgia. The contributions of these gifted education specialists helped to refine the study and suggest many new ideas and challenges. These suggestions are reflected in Heller's research (see *Formen der Hochbegabung Bei Kindern und Jugendlichen: Identifikation, Entwicklungsund Listungsanalyse 1984a).*

West Germany is just beginning to experiment with the idea of giftedness. However, it has chosen to educate the gifted within the traditional confines of its existing system — offering few special provisions.

England and Wales

The concept of giftedness lacks precise definition in England and Wales. Many overlapping definitions of giftedness (Wallace 1985) exist in spite of (or perhaps because of) the fact that many gifted research projects have been conducted (Department of Education and Science 1967; Shields 1968; Pringle 1970; Hitchfield 1973; Ogilvie 1973; Burt 1974; Taylor, Reid, and Holley 1974; Department of Education and Science Library 1975; Hoyle and Wilks 1975; Freeman 1976; Painter 1976). Many British educators and policymakers have identified the sixth form, a highly specialized program of the academically superior (one to three years before university admission), as appropriate and sufficient training for the gifted. This excellent program, however, does not address the depth and breadth of gifted needs. In addition, it fails to speak to the issue of neglect. In strongly egalitarian schools, teachers refuse to identify gifted children because they worry that such a practice could contribute to a elite cadre, and in schools occupied with other pressing concerns, educators are indifferent to the needs of gifted children and assume the gifted children can make it on their own. But in these countries, according to the working party report of the Department of Education and Science in 1977, the most typical orientation differs from both these approaches. The report said, ''Most schools were neither reluctant to consider giftedness nor indifferent to the matter. The plain fact was that 'giftedness' as a concept had not been thought about'' (Department of Education and Science 1977, p. 9).

Few teachers in these schools have any awareness of the criteria used to identify giftedness. Gifted children are often identified accidentally by an external agency program, including Local Educational Agency (LEA) pilot testing, museum programs, local affiliates of the National Association of Gifted Children, and national competitions. Parents of gifted children with high expectations — particularly in middle-class communities — compel schools to recognize the need of gifted children, and maladjusted or disruptive gifted children often force the school system to recognize their needs. Schools that are required to recognize gifted needs by LEAs also exist (see Marjoram, in press, for LEA requirements and approaches in England, outside full-time education and employment). Finally, some schools are accustomed to identifying giftedness. However, the manner in which such children are identified is rarely consistent or systematic (see Maltby, in press, concerning teacher identification of gifted). Gifted children in England and Wales are often treated as individual problems rather than as a group with special needs. " 'Slow learners,' in contrast, are provided for as a problem group. Whereas gifted children can work below their potential from lack of challenge or from personal choice, and pass unnoticed, slow learners can less easily disguise their inability to work at the level and pace of their fellows'' (Department of Education and Science 1977, p. 13).

Some middle and comprehensive secondary schools have policies and procedures for identifying gifted children (see King 1962, pp. 192–203 for a description of middle and comprehensive secondary schools). Unfortunately, such policies are erratic, and the identification practices are employed haphazardly. The typical approach to identifying gifted children is teacher recommendation. This practice is highly dependent on the special expertise and time of the teacher. (See Postlethwaite and Denton 1983 about improvements in this area.) In addition, primary school records help place students in secondary schools. This practice is useful and effective — when primary school staff and secondary staff are familiar with each other's programs and agree on the meaning of student records. Unfortunately, records and exemplary achievements that suggest potential giftedness are often overlooked.

Most secondary schools use group intelligence tests during the first year to place students in the school system. The Manchester Grammar School in Great Britain, for example, requires "the necessary standard in the competitive entrance examination'' for admission (Stone 1965). However, few schools use intelligence tests to identify gifted children. In fact, some schools refuse to use intelligence tests to avoid self-fulfilling prophecies. Attempts are being made to make the screening process more systematic. Headmasters are taking a more active role in sensitizing their staff and parents to early identification of the gifted. Periodic reviews of student progress, during any given year and at critical transition points, have increasingly been geared to identify unusually high intellectual performers. These efforts are promising. However, the current overall approach to identification in England and Wales is inconsistent and routinely results in lost opportunities for gifted children.

Middle and comprehensive secondary schools in these countries provide a variety of instructional approaches for the gifted. For example, they use *streaming*, which is similar to tracking. Students are placed in separate classes according to general ability, and gifted students are often placed in top or express streams. Unfortunately, most gifted students require a more advanced level and pace than the top streams offer. *Setting* means grouping students according to specific ability or achievement. For example, exceptional performers in mathematics may be placed together in the highest set. The Maesydderwen Comprehensive School in Wales has an international reputation for its success with the setting approach (Thomas 1965). *Mixed-ability grouping* combines students of high and low academic ability. This type of approach rarely challenges the gifted child: A mixed-ability class is often geared to the mean.

The ability of the teacher to provide differentiation (compared with a conventional "whole-class teaching method") is an important element common to all these approaches. Streaming, setting, and mixed-ability grouping are all potentially appropriate approaches to educating the gifted child. However, successful instruction in each of these grouping approaches depends on the teacher's ability. Successful gifted teachers are able to guide students at different levels of abstraction depending on their ability and interest. Effective teachers can provide a setting for student-programmed instructional projects in any of these grouping approaches.

A *pull-out* approach is also used similar to the approach used in the United States. Students are withdrawn from their classes during the school day to receive special training. Typically, a gifted musician leaves regular classes to receive special instruction. In some cases, foreign language training is available. Students must make up any lost material during special training sessions after school. All-around gifted students or those with high general intellectual ability may be promoted to the next higher grade or age grouping. A decision to promote a gifted child is highly dependent on the child's maturity level and general social coping skills. Acceleration involves advancement in individual subjects. A gifted physicist may take science courses beyond his or her chronological peers, yet continue English studies with students of his or her own age. This arrangement is particularly rare because of the organizational difficulties it poses for schools.

Enrichment is as loose a term in England and Wales as it is in the United States. It often becomes a catchall term for any supplementary instruction, ranging from field trips to additional homework.

Enrichment ideally involves qualitatively different work — not more of the same (see *Public Schools Commission Second Report* 1970). Enrichment activities typically require a level of abstraction above and beyond the established curriculum. "Enrichment materials can be as general as extensive library facilities, but usually they are in the form of curriculum development material designed to improve the quality of thinking. In this sense, only one example of enrichment material was seen" in England and Wales by the Department of Education and Science Working Party (1977, p. 29). However, Ogilvie's (1980) council curriculum enrichment project and Callow's (1982) Council Gifted Pupils project represent important contributions to curriculum enrichment development in England. In addition, promising work is being conducted in the area of curriculum enrichment by the British Association in the County of Clevand (Adams 1985). (See also Print 1983; and Foster 1983.)

Other provisions for the gifted student outside the school include transfer to another institution, partial transfer, local education authority programs, mentors, and parents. Students with exceptional musical ability, for example, may be transferred to an institution with a particularly strong music program. In some cases, only partial transfer is necessary or appropriate. Students may be able to study a particular topic that is not available in the home school at another institution for a few hours each day. The Brentwood College of Education, which offered half-day classes for gifted students, was one of the more successful experiments in partial transfer (Bridges 1969). The local educational authorities may subsidize these transfers or provide support for specialized instruction in the arts. Mentors — although difficult to schedule and match to student interests — periodically work with gifted students on advanced projects. As in the United States, parents of the gifted in England and Wales provide special expertise, encouragement, and high expectations.

England and Wales, like Germany, primarily serve gifted children through their existing educational systems. However, these countries have developed a slightly more sophisticated, albeit erratic, approach to the gifted than has Germany, using special grouping, tracking, pull-out, and enrichment approaches. One of the most positive telling aspects of the English and Welsh systems is the use of mentors and the apparent ease of transferring exceptional students to appropriate institutions for special instruction.

Canada

Canada, like most countries, is not monolithic in its orientation toward the gifted. Each province has a different level of commitment to the gifted. The most supportive provinces outshine England and Wales's approach to the gifted, ranging from policies to actual programs. In fact, many of its programs are based on American models. However, in provinces where little support exists, benign neglect governs the educational system for the gifted.

Canada has ten provinces with various gifted policies and practices. It is increasingly more interested in gifted education but still not highly supportive of it. The Canadian Educational Association study found "that not one department/ministry of education had grants specifically earmarked for the education of these [gifted] students" (Borthwick et al. 1980, p. 37). Instead, financial support comes from special funds or special education funding.

British Columbia's Ministry of Education has a policy that supports programs for the gifted; its legal provision for gifted programs is cited under the Public Schools Act. Ontario recognizes the need to serve gifted children and emphasizes the fact that "teachers are responsible for providing each child with the opportunity to achieve levels of competence commensurate with ability" (Ontario Ministry of Education 1978, p. 2). Regulation seven of the Education Act of 1974 provides legislative support for gifted programs. Quebec leaves the responsibility of educating the gifted to local school boards on an as-needed basis. Nova Scotia's government encourages school administrators to meet the needs of gifted children, ranging from the academically gifted to the athletically capable student. But although individual enrichment programs receive support, no special classses or courses are available. Local school systems have the responsibility of identifying the needs of the gifted in place of any formal legislation. Prince Edward Island's policy supports a "broad educational program" modified for the gifted to include individualized programs and subject area acceleration. Prince Edward Island does not have specific legislation that supports gifted education. Newfoundland does not have a formal educational policy for the gifted. However, schools are encouraged to identify and meet the needs of the gifted. Newfoundland also lacks any gifted legislation. In Alberta, "gifted pupils are usually accommodated within the regular program" (Borthwick et al. 1980, p. 38). No legal

provision exists for the establishment of gifted programs. Saskatchewan does not have an educational policy for gifted and talented programs, but legal provision for the gifted derives from the
Education Act of 1978. Manitoba does not have specific legislation
authorizing the establishment of gifted education, but its educational
policy allows schools to develop their own programs. New Brunswick
also lacks an official policy and legislation to support the gifted.

This inconsistency and ambivalence to gifted education is also
evident in other areas. No required qualifications exist for teachers
of the gifted in any provinces. Only Ontario, Quebec, and Nova Scotia
provide funds for gifted and talented program needs related to
transportation. In-service training is available in only half the
provinces: British Columbia, Alberta, Saskatchewan, Ontario, and
New Brunswick. Only British Columbia and Ontario conduct research
and evaluation of gifted programs. Very little curriculum development takes place throughout Canada on the provincial level, except in
Ontario *(Gifted/Talented Children* 1978) and British Columbia.
Typically, school boards develop their own curricula and distribute
teaching material throughout the district.

Canadian provinces also use varying definitions and methods for
identifying and selecting gifted and talented children. Generally,
however, gifted children are defined as the top 2 to 3 percent of the
population. Most often, the principal is responsible for admitting
students into gifted and talented programs. However, the resource
teacher is most frequently assigned the responsibility of administering
the program.

Categories to identify gifted children in various provinces
include intellectual, artistic, psychomotor, and leadership categories.
Teacher selection is the method most frequently used to identify gifted
children — despite the body of evidence indicating that this method
is ineffectual and inconsistent. Teacher selection often works in
conjunction with group and individual intelligence tests. According
to Borthwick et al. (1980, p. 57), parent and peer selection appear
to be the lowest-rated methods of identifying the gifted.

Multiple criteria exist for the identification and selection of gifted
and talented students. High performance is the most frequently used
criterion. In addition, a student usually requires a specific IQ to gain
admittance to most programs; the range is from 115 to 145, and an
average of 130 is considered acceptable or appropriate.

The educational approaches available in Canada parallel many of the approaches in the United States. In fact, many Canadian programs are based on U.S. models, including the Project for the Academically Talented of the National Educational Association (see Laycock 1962, pp. 230, 231; see also Getzels and Jackson 1960). School boards throughout Canada provide special schools, special classes, ability grouping, and acceleration for gifted children. In addition, enrichment, weekend classes, and independent study are available. Only a few special schools for the gifted exist in Canada. The few existing special schools and classes provide homogeneous group settings for gifted students. These approaches allow gifted children to work at their own pace with their intellectual peers, and they also help teachers target the needs of the gifted. In addition, such instructional organization provides a convincing rationale at school board meetings for hiring specially trained gifted teachers. Canadian educators, like educators throughout the world, report worries that these approaches will foster elitism and "promote snobbery." In addition, a concern exists that regular classes may lose an important resource.

Ability grouping is the most common approach for gifted Canadian children. Gifted students are grouped according to achievement, interest, and intellectual potential within special or conventional classrooms. This approach narrows the intellectual range of the classroom, enabling the teacher to focus attention on the individual needs of students within the same general intellectual spectrum. The individualized nature of this approach, however, can pose scheduling and evaluation problems.

Gifted students can be accelerated by skipping grades or by completing courses in a topic area at a rapid pace. These practices allow students to pursue their interests according to their own timetable. In addition, acceleration enables students to complete their studies in a shorter period of time. It also prevents boredom. Problems that result from skipping grades include educational gaps and emotional difficulty.

Canadian schools also provide vertical and horizontal enrichment programs. Vertical programs allow students to study subjects beyond their own grade level. Students can complete their education at a faster pace with vertical enrichment programs. In addition, as is the case with acceleration, vertical programs allow students to explore knowledge at their own pace, alleviating boredom in the process.

The disadvantages of vertical enrichment include potential learning gaps and emotional problems. Horizontal programs broaden the students' capabilities on the same grade level. This approach allows students to specialize in an area of interest; however, it may represent a double-edged sword. Specialization at an early age may erect obstacles to broad-based education, and horizontal enrichment programs may stifle a gifted student's desire to explore knowledge in a vertical growth pattern.

Independent study programs have been successful instructional approaches for motivated gifted children. Students typically work under the guidance of one individual, such as the teacher, and use a variety of resources, including library journals, texts, and experts. Independent study programs enable the student to investigate independently and in depth a particular interest (see Project Equity 1973). Independent study programs typically minimize supervision. As in the United States, Canadian students who lack sufficient internal motivation often flounder in such programs. Evaluating an independent study course can pose a problem.

Canada's provincial governments delegate the responsibility of educating their children to the local school boards. A view of the local school board level provides the best picture of how Canada serves the gifted. According to the Canadian Educational Association study (Borthwick et al. 1980), only 37 percent of respondents in their survey made special provisions for the gifted and talented. In addition, only 26.1 percent of respondents stated that they had a specific policy for the gifted and talented. These figures may be overly conservative, since they do not account for individual schools or teachers who assume this responsibility. Moreover, they do not capture the role of private school programs. Nevertheless, they do indicate a weakness in the Canadian educational system.

Acceleration, in Canada, is determined on an individual basis. School boards appear split in their attitude toward this practice, so the decision generally hinges on the child's social, psychological, and physical maturity. The most typical gifted and talented offerings in Canada are enrichment programs. The programs, ranging from the most frequent to least frequent, include independent study, part-time classes, resource centers, special subjects, tutorial assistance, full-time classes, summer programs, weekend programs, after-school programs, and special schools. In one study, special full-time classes had the highest numbers of enrolled students, followed by part-time classes and weekend programs (see Borthwick et al. 1980, p. 63).

Israel

Israel's Ministry of Education and Culture is centralized in Jerusalem, with branches in six regions throughout the country. The ministry shares its educational responsibilities with local educational authorities. It is active in the full range of educational activities, including the selection of personnel, distribution of salaries, in-service training, and curriculum development.

Department for Gifted Children

The Ministry of Education and Culture has a Department for Gifted Children. Provision for establishing this department derived from the first minister's position "that each child has the right to develop his abilities and that it is the task of the Ministry to provide proper frameworks and content, which will enable such development" (Burg 1985, p. 4). The department serves an important coordination function across the country and provides new directions in the field.

The Department for Gifted Children was established in 1971 — in spite of Israel's strong "egalitarian educational philosophy" (Burg 1985) — and began operating in 1972. The department's stated purpose "is to identify the most able pupils on a countrywide scale, to develop teachers' sensitivity for the needs of special pupils in their classes, and to prepare programs for classes and enrichment centers covering a scope of academic interests" (Burg 1985, p. 4). According to the former director,

> There is no doubt that the establishment of this department contributed to the intensification of action: there are more places in Israel where these children are being taken care of, more kinds of action have been developed, more research is being done. Moreover, prejudices are lessening and the subject is gradually turning from a "foster child," struggling for its existence in the educational system, to a recognized problem which one should relate to and try to find solutions for. (Bitan 1976, p. 323)

Special provisions are made for the gifted with general intellectual ability or specific academic aptitude throughout the country. Students must take qualifying examinations to participate in gifted and talented programs. The Ortar test is used most frequently, and the WISC scale is drawing increasing interest.

Programs

Israel has successfully experimented with in-school, special class enrichment programs. Students receive six hours of special classroom instruction per week, yet remain in their home school. This type of approach is becoming increasingly popular throughout the country. (See Burg, Or-Noy, and Taitel, in press, concerning the Ofek School in Jerusalem.)

Children are tested for admittance into all-day special classes in grade two. Gifted students require a mean IQ of 143 (Bitan 1976, p. 325). Selected students participate in this program in grade three. They are taught in neighborhood schools or, when necessary, are transferred from their homes to continue their education in this setting until sixth grade, or until they complete secondary school. Israel has thirteen such special classes for gifted children. Some parents have expressed their concern about the social isolation their children might experience if they enroll in special classes (see Burg 1984).

In addition, morning and afternoon enrichment programs are available. Morning enrichment programs provide full-day instruction once a week for gifted children. Typically, gifted children attend morning enrichment programs at a different institution from their neighborhood school and spend the remainder of the week receiving instruction in their neighborhood school. More than fifteen separate institutions provide after-school enrichment programs for the gifted at the elementary school level. Gifted students attend special courses twice a week in the sciences, humanities, and arts. These programs are not part of the school system but belong to university, museum, and other educational entities. University affiliate programs offer such facilities as laboratories, computer centers, and sophisticated libraries.

Israel has taken steps to identify gifted students from low socioeconomic classes and minorities. Successful efforts include "post elementary boarding schools for able disadvantaged, whose social conditions at home are difficult and/or there is not an appropriate school in the place of their residence" (Bitan 1976, p. 326). The Welfare Programs and Renewal Projects Department provide for the gifted from lower socioeconomic levels. In addition, the Weizmann

Institute has provided scholarships for students who will serve as tutors for the disenfranchised (Bitan 1976, p. 326).

Curriculum

The curriculum in special classes includes advanced course material, an enriched regular curriculum, and a specially designed curriculum. The specially designed curriculum consists of the regular curriculum, combined with topics such as astrophysics and electronics. Curriculum inspectors are currently placing greater emphasis on "integrating the different domains of knowledge" in gifted classes, including flexibility and emphasizing divergent thinking. Although the curriculum is flexible, the ministry does not encourage acceleration.

Israel has a national educational center with a department specifically focused on the gifted. However, like Canada, the degree of commitment to the gifted varies from one district to the next. In addition to its special class enrichment programs, all-day special classes, and various in-school enrichment programs, Israel is noted for its after-school enrichment programs and its serious attempt to identify gifted minority students.

Japan

Japan does not have or recognize any formal gifted and talented education program in its public educational system. The culture as a whole is concerned about allowing any student to stand out from the group and to jeopardize the perception of equity. However, private elementary schools track students for admission into private prestigious universities. In addition, students in public school are required to take an entrance examination for admission to high school (grades ten to twelve). The higher the score, the greater the likelihood of gaining entrance into a selective academic track high school; average scores result in admission to less competitive schools, and low scores deny access to a college preparatory high school. Schools rather than classes in schools are tracked. As in Germany, England, and Wales, the Japanese approach to the gifted is very much a part of the existing school system.

Periodic government reports call for educational reform, emphasizing the need to attend to creativity, but they have not been effective in altering the existing (nationally sponsored) public educational system. The Japanese educational system is recognized for producing a highly educated citizenry in general, although it is not known for uncommon individual efforts. (See Rohlen 1983 for a description of the Japanese secondary school system; see also Cummings 1980; Kirst 1981; Singleton 1967; Torrance 1980; and Vogel 1979.) In general, then, Japan, unlike Israel and most other countries, does not recognize the gifted. However, its high school entrance examinations serve to track students as effectively as many gifted programs.

Conclusion

A variety of studies on gifted and talented education are being conducted throughout the world. Three of the most promising are in the Philippines, in China, and in Israel.

The College of Education in the University of the Philippines is currently conducting a study of gifted and talented programs throughout the country. Its research focuses on the Philippine Science High School, the National School for the Arts, and the Silahis Center. The results should be available within two years. See also the report on the survey of The Fifth World Conference participants from the Asian/Pacific region and the Philippines (Roldan, in press).

The Chinese have recently adopted Western models to accomplish many of their educational reforms (Lin 1985, pp. 1, 28). Their shift in approach also extends to the gifted. The Chinese have been conducting a six-year nationwide study of more than one hundred gifted or superior children ranging in age from three to sixteen years (Zha, in press). In addition, they have conducted comparative studies with more than five thousand normal children. Based on this research, "several special classes for supernormal children have been established" (Zha, in press). Zha (in press) has identified a number of developmental conditions associated with the gifted:

1. Good family environment and education provide good bases for these children's development.
2. Suitable school education is the key condition for the further development of supernormal children (these children benefit from many extra activities, a variety of competitions, and so on).
3. Some personality characteristics are important or essential.

These conditions correspond with research findings on American gifted children.

The Israeli head of the Pedagogical Secretariate in the Ministry of Education and Culture and the Director of the Department for Gifted Children are currently discussing Israel's developing gifted programs with the author, focusing on identification practices, curriculum development, and the role of the lower socioeconomic class gifted child.

Programs for and the studies of gifted and talented education have been developed throughout the world. The Soviet Union is experimenting successfully with boarding schools, special schools, and in-class enrichment programs. In addition, it has developed one of the most elaborate after-school enrichment programs in the world. Australia demonstrates a variety of attitudes about the gifted, ranging from supportive to obstructive. Australian approaches include enrichment, school clusters, special interest centers, gifted classes and schools, and acceleration. New Zealand's educational policies are strongly egalitarian in nature. However, successful local efforts have taken place in developing gifted programs.

West Germany's efforts to develop gifted programs are still in their infancy. Its program for the gifted is essentially an artifact of its existing educational system. Heller's research represents an exciting development in German gifted education. His six-year longitudinal study will shed light on identification criteria for the gifted.

The concept of giftedness is imprecise in England and Wales. However, middle and comprehensive secondary schools have policies and procedures for the identification of gifted children. Useful approaches include streaming, setting, and mixed-ability grouping. Each approach depends on the teacher's ability to provide a differentiated educational experience. In addition, pull-out programs, acceleration, and enrichment classes are available. Other provisions include institutional transfer, partial transfer, local educational programs, mentors, and parents.

Canada has grown increasingly interested in the development of gifted education. Policies, practices, definitions, and methods of identification vary considerably from one province to another. The most typical categories for identifying gifted children across provinces include intellectual, artistic, psychomotor, and leadership categories. The educational approaches available in Canada parallel many of those in the Unites States — including special schools, special classes, ability grouping, acceleration, and enrichment. Israel has successfully experimented with in-school special-class enrichment activities, all-day special classes, and enrichment programs. Finally, Japan, although it does not formally recognize the gifted, has selective public high schools that track students for academic success in selective universities.

This brief review of gifted and talented programs throughout the world is reassuring. Programs and policies share a precarious position across the globe. Nevertheless, nations appear to recognize the value of the gifted and talented in spite of strong opposing ideological dispositions. (See World Conference on Gifted and Talented Education volumes for additional cross-cultural material about the gifted, including Cropley et al., in press.)

By providing an international overview of gifted and talented education, this chaper has placed our own educational system in a cross-cultural perspective. These comparisons in some instances give us reason to congratulate ourselves; in many others, it forces us to pause and recognize how far we lag behind and how much more work lies ahead. In this light, the concluding chapter warns of the dangers of educational complacency and neglect in a global economy. The conclusion points to the role and value of gifted education in our effort to restore education nationwide. A model of excellence derives from useful elements or features of successful programs examined throughout this work — at home and abroad. The model is designed to help strengthen our entire educational system. Finally, a call is made for the revitalization of gifted and talented education throughout the United States — beginning with the establishment of a national center.

CHAPTER 7

Toward a Model of Excellence

The future of our nation lies in the minds of our children. Education is one of the most powerful cultural tools available to convey content, transmit values, and stimulate imaginations. The quality of young minds is dependent on the quality of education that they experience.

> We . . . need to make a much clearer and more emphatic commitment to excellence and to its nurturing throughout the educational system. We have paid a good deal of attention, over the past decade and a half, to problems of access — to the important business of making sure that those who can make use of educational opportunity have a chance at it. That is an important item on our social agenda, and we must not forget it. But neither can we afford to forget our obligations to the very brightest and most capable students — the ones who can provide path-breaking leadership in the future. The decline of mathematics and science programs in secondary schools, the filling-up of school curricula with optional subject-matter that is not very relevant to academic development, the shifting away of financial aid programs from highest performers to average performers — all these are signs that indicate that too little attention is being paid to the development of unusual potential (Kennedy 1985, p. 8).

Gifted and talented children and able learners (Cox, Daniel, and Boston 1985) have a right to equal educational opportunity. The gifted stand at the margins of an educational system geared toward the mean. According to one conventional definition of giftedness, intellectually gifted children constitute the top 3 percent of the population — a group of the same size as that labelled "mentally retarded." The gifted have special needs much like the handicapped. "Although society generally recognizes the needs of students who are physically or mentally handicapped and is therefore willing to make special education provisions for them, the needs of students who deviate upward from the mean have been generally untended'' (California State Department of Education 1979). Gifted students are often placed in lock-step programs. Special programs are needed to foster their potential and to enable them to make productive contributions to society (Tannenbaum 1983).

Contrary to popular expectation, gifted children will not make it on their own. Only half the gifted children in the United States have been identified as gifted. Approximately one-third of these identified children participate in gifted programs. Those students in regular classrooms lack the stimulation to challenge their intellect and draw their interest. Boredom in the classroom can turn to disillusionment, underachievement, disruption, and lost potential.

Educational neglect is a hidden time bomb in the United States. U.S. success in global competition depends on the gifts and talents of the next generation of scientists, scholars, artists, athletes, and leaders. We cannot afford the price of national complacency. In *The Fifth Generation: Artificial Intelligence and Japan's Computer Challenge to the World*, Feigenbaum and McCorduck (1983) describe our precarious position in the global economy, where ''knowledge itself is to become the new wealth of nations'' (p. xvi). They discuss the Japanese Ministry of International Trade and Industry's ten-year plan to develop knowledge information processing systems. They also discuss the effects of our technological complacency.

We now regret our complacency in other technologies. Who in the 1960s took seriously the Japanese initiative in small cars? Who in 1970 took seriously the Japanese national goal to become number one in consumer electronics in ten years? (Have you seen an American VCR that isn't Japanese on the inside?) In 1972, when the Japanese had yet to produce their first commercial microelectronic chip but announced their national plans in this vital ''made in America'' technology, who would have thought that in ten years they would have half of the world's market for the most advanced memory chips? Are we about to blow it again? The consequences of complacency, of our spirited attention to the near-in at the expense of the long view, will be devastating to the economic health of our most important industry. Even more important than its direct effect on the computing industry, present complacency will have serious economic effects on all industries. Since computing is the technology that drives all other technologies, a second-rate computing industry will also mean impaired industrial design and manufacturing, and enfeebled management and planning. The Japanese could thereby become the dominant industrial power in the world. (p.xvii)

The gifted and the able learner have a major role to play in our international competition, in the computer field and elsewhere. A shortsighted view of their needs will have long-term effects on us as a nation much as our technological complacency has jeopardized our position in the world today. SAT scores, which had dropped in recent years, are beginning to climb again and many political proclamations have been made about our return to excellence. But these superficial signs of our time should not distract us from the serious work ahead. We cannot afford to be lulled into a false sense of security and, thus, into stagnation and complacency.

Gifted education also provides a model to revive our entire educational system. Local gifted programs have already helped raise standards of the regular school system in the areas of student performance, curriculum development, teaching, and administration. Gifted and talented teachers provide an excellent pool of educators from which to select master or lead teachers to improve the teaching profession in response to the Carnegie Task Force Report on Teaching as a Profession. Increasingly, local school boards, superintendents, and principals have been reevaluating the value of their gifted programs as the pressures to improve the quality of education are translated into the practical and political realities of higher scholastic scores.

A Model of Excellence

Gifted and talented education can serve as a beacon for the entire educational community. An evaluation of more than 433 domestic gifted and talented education programs and a review of programs throughout the world, including the Soviet Union, suggest that successful gifted and talented education programs offer a model of academic and administrative excellence that is generalizable to the mainstream of the American educational system.This review of successful programs identified several key elements worthy of adoption, including quality, commitment, leadership, diversity of curriculum and instruction, and a whole-person approach (see Fetterman 1984c). This model is a distillation and integration of the most significant attributes of successful gifted programs discussed in the preceding review of programs. Many of the model's elements characterize precisely those conditions that — according to the Richardson study of MacArthur Fellows — encourage inquiry, originality, self-directedness, and creativity (Cox, Daniel, and Boston 1985, p. 12). The conditions, highlighted in the Richardson study, include significant teachers, high expectations, acceleration and flexible instruction, special educational opportunities, and supportive parents (pp. 12–28).

Quality

Quality is a scarce and undervalued commodity in American society. Declining test scores, illiterate high school graduates, increasing violence, and growing in-school truancy are all manifestations of a decline in the quality of our educational system. Gifted and talented classrooms are characterized by the highest test scores and some of the most advanced or accelerated instruction in the nation. Discussions are enthusiastic, in-depth, and well researched, and virtually no reported violence or in-school truancy takes place in the gifted and talented classroom. Students are eager to come to class, and teachers and students share a commitment to the pursuit of excellence in teaching and learning.

High expectations form an essential ingredient of gifted and talented programs. Administrators, teachers, and parents maintain high expectations about gifted programs and student achievement. Both teachers and students are under constant pressure to perform. At the same time that teachers are recognized as the authority in the classroom, they need to be able to admit that they do not know everything. Gifted teachers work to draw out the qualities students bring to the classroom as well as to impart knowledge. They typically engage the student in a dialogue throughout their studies, following what I call a "blossoming approach" to educational instruction. Students respect and admire these teachers as authority figures, facilitators, and general resources. In this atmosphere, students are willing to take risks in front of their teachers and peers.

Gifted students internalize the values of open inquiry. They learn to develop their own standards of excellence and to hold themselves to those internal standards and ideals. The concept of improvement remains open-ended and lifelong, and a strong belief exists that there is always room for improvement. The students are able to maintain these high expectations because gifted programs operate in a meritocracy, where quality work is recognized and rewarded and mediocrity is frowned upon. Gifted and talented teachers do not reinforce average work, and gifted students rarely let banal comments pass in a classroom discussion. This insistence on quality produces a classroom climate of intellectual challenge and stimulation.

Gifted and talented programs are designed to provide a qualitatively different educational experience. The aim is to provide both vertical and horizontal educational opportunities. In other words, such programs build on — as well as supplement — the core curriculum. Unique opportunities are an important part of any successful gifted and talented program. In a typical program, students studying Elizabethan drama present a semiprofessional theatrical performance in addition to preparing term papers and taking tests. The money earned from their performances enables them to visit the Shakespeare Festival in Ashland, Oregon. The entire experience is interwoven with the curriculum — an improvement over the piecemeal conglomeration of experiences that too often characterizes education. Other gifted students interested in marine biology and oceanography complete classroom activities designed to solve specific problems, such as water pollution. They study each problem, develop hypotheses, and then conduct research on a floating laboratory to test their hypotheses. In another program, students studying astronomy have been offered the opportunity to re-create a space lab and to attend lectures by prominent scientific and science fiction writers, such as Carl Sagan and Ray Bradbury. A program in the Midwest offers students interested in archaeology an opportunity to discover artifacts on an archaeological dig in addition to their regular studies. In another instance, students in elementary gifted and talented programs are building windmills that generate electricity. Junior high school students are developing and operating a model United Nations. High school students are involved in model city-planning activities. These programs are aimed at the synthesis and evaluation levels of learning — the higher cognitive levels of Bloom's taxonomy. These types of experiences increase the quality of the learning experience and the program rather than simply adding to the quantity of schoolwork.

In their efforts to improve education, the National Commission on Excellence in Education recommended (1983) either a longer school day or a lengthened school year. The commission's intention is praiseworthy, but its recommendation is off target. Levin (1984) makes a cogent argument questioning the wisdom of this type of recommendation from an economic perspective. He suggests that our focus should be on the quality — not the quantity — of time our children spend in intellectual pursuits. (See also Stedman and Smith 1983 concerning problems with commission recommendations.) Gifted and talented programs prove this point routinely in their part-time enrichment programs. Many gifted and talented programs have little time — often only two hours a day — to educate and illuminate young minds. Time must be used effectively and efficiently if the program is to have any merit. The teachers are able to provide an optimum amount of material in a short time and still stimulate imaginations, and students learn to engage themselves in their materials almost immediately. The aim for all parties concerned is not simply to pass time, but to do the best with the time available.

Commitment

Quality requires commitment. Teachers in gifted programs are dedicated and conscientious educators, engaging in classroom preparation as rigorously as in classroom presentation to maximize the time with the children. Collaboration with colleagues and professionals outside the community is common. Teachers in gifted programs are also concerned with the whole person and recognize that the students' personal lives have a direct effect on their school life. Most teachers in gifted programs enthusiastically invite parent consultation and are often deeply involved in extracurricular student activities without additional compensation. This involvement may range from theatrical presentations demanding weeks of after-school rehearsal time to the many scrimmages necessary for athletic competition in tournaments.

Students are committed to completing their individual tasks and assignments with the highest performance level possible. They take their classroom work seriously and routinely request (and require) additional after-school projects. Individual commitment to excellence is contagious. A positive peer pressure to perform can generalize throughout a program. Students can also act as a quality control, since they are fast to respond to inadequate teacher performance, informing the teacher immediately if the lesson is off target or if it is aimed significantly below their capabilities. Gifted students are not reluctant to inform other parties about a problem with classroom instruction if it cannot be resolved with the teacher involved.

Parents also demonstrate a commitment to their children's education unparalleled in the American educational system. Such parents are actively engaged in assessing the quality of the education their children receive, and continually and often aggressively monitor their children's progress. They ask their children specifically what they are doing and how well they are doing in each category of schoolwork. They uninhibitedly consult with teachers and administration about the quality of instruction and about the academic progress of their child. Parents devote much time to working with their children on individual school assignments and projects. Moreover, they contribute much to their children's preparation. Many parents of gifted children teach them to read before they enter kindergarten. Most of these parents continue to provide academic instruction in the home throughout elementary and secondary school, as well as time and resources to supplement their children's education. Their help may range from providing funding for special academically oriented summer camps to volunteering time to assist the teacher during the school day.

Parents of gifted children are also actively engaged in the political education arena. They generally play a large part in parent-teacher organizations and routinely become involved in district and state politics concerning matters related to gifted educational instruction programs. Threats to the quality of the program, such as funding cuts or curriculum alterations, elicit an overwhelming public forum of concerned, articulate parents.

Gifted program administrators also demonstrate a tremendous devotion to gifted programs. Often these administrators work only part-time for the gifted program while they assume a number of other unrelated activities, including the administration of additional programs. Given the typically low funding for gifted programs, an administrator must be extremely creative and resourceful to ensure that the program maintains its high standards and that the integrity of the program model is not violated. Gifted administrators must work constantly to maintain existing funds and to search for additional supplementary funds to cover the expenses of innovative curriculum improvements. They continually seek new gifted teachers to sustain and enrich the program. Moreover, they need to be particularly adept at coordinating services throughout the district and at balancing the political interests that shape district decision making.

Leadership

Educational leadership is an integral component of any successful education program or system. The quality of leadership determines whether the program will sail smoothly on course or drift aimlessly and perhaps crash on rocky shores. Commitment overlaps with leadership in gifted education. Administrators must demonstrate commitment and superior leadership qualities to be successful. They must be able to provide district- or statewide direction for their gifted program. This direction requires knowledge of the latest legislative developments and administrative policies that may affect gifted education programs. Moreover, gifted administrators must be willing and able to navigate through murky and often politically treacherous waters. Leadership also requires self-confidence and a sense of humor under pressure. Administrators of successful gifted programs possess all these characteristics. They tend to be charismatic individuals with a vision and a plan for the future.

The role of the principal or coordinator of a gifted program is also instrumental to its success. This individual is in a position to shape, coordinate, and reinforce the guiding principles of the program. He or she ensures that principles of organization, independent responsibility, and self-reliance, among others, are reinforced in the curriculum and in each classroom. Principals and coordinators of gifted programs command parental, teacher, and student support and respect by communicating a clear sense of direction and by providing periodic reports on measurable goals and objectives.

Parents of gifted children also demonstrate the significance of leadership in the educational system. They typically assume leadership positions in the community ranging from participation in the board of education to official positions in parent-teacher organizations. Many are active on state and local government levels as well. These role models serve to reinforce the importance of leadership and civic responsibility for their children.

Students also assume strong leadership roles in the school and the community. They are encouraged to assume leadership responsibilities at an early age—for example, to run for class president or school newspaper director, or to develop their own computer software company. Gifted curricula are often designed to draw out and refine leadership qualities with team projects, classroom presentations, and science fair activities.

Diversity of Curriculum and Instruction

Gifted programs are designed to meet the individual needs of gifted children (see Plowman 1969 and Fetterman, in press). A well-thought-out, sequential curriculum represents the baseline of any successful gifted and talented program. Effective gifted teachers are able to relate enthusiastic discussions to the program's sequential curriculum. Within some boundaries, gifted students are allowed to work at their own pace on a number of projects. In addition, a broad range of courses are available. These courses are presented in a variety of ways because most gifted teachers recognize that no single instructional technique works for all children. Special activities broaden the knowledge base of the course materials. For example, students often have the opportunity to participate in projects that supplement classroom instruction, such as marine biology experiments at nearby marine stations and theatrical performances in local repertory theaters. In addition, mentors or professionals in the community are sought out to work with children who have similar interests. Students are also given opportunities to study languages in foreign countries and to participate in archaeological excavations. These activities stimulate and reinforce learning and are carefully selected and shaped to reinforce and expand the existing school curriculum.

The Whole-Person Approach

One of the most significant tools in gifted and talented programs is the whole-person approach (see Fetterman 1981), which is frequently used in programs for dropouts and disabled children. The whole-person approach requires teachers to address both the personal and the academic concerns of children. Personal factors inhibit or encourage academic achievement. Gifted teachers serve as counselors as well as educators, and teachers take an active role in assisting gifted children through their psychosocial development. They may help students organize their personal lives by demonstrating how to establish priorities and timetables. In many instances, teachers may simply lend a friendly ear, listening to student problems and frustrations regarding adjustment to peers, physical development, and familial problems. Gifted teachers recognize that personal problems manifest themselves in academic performance, and effective gifted educators address their students' personal problems directly to facilitate the personal and academic growth of each gifted child. (See also Zaffrann 1978; and Colangelo and Zaffrann 1979 concerning counseling the gifted.) Most gifted teachers are also actively involved in their students' extracurricular activities, including sports, scouting, and various special projects. These teachers are often viewed as friends as well as teachers by gifted children. Thus a strong mutual personal bond develops in a healthy gifted environment. Teachers often invite their students to parties at their homes, and teachers and students are able to joke with each other without detracting from their respective social roles and jeopardizing their educational relationship.

Generalizable Traits

Our educational system needs revitalizing in many areas. Gifted and talented education programs in the United States, however, provide one of the best places to begin the ascent toward excellence in education. Tannenbaum (1983) describes the success of the magnet school concept, in which gifted and talented education programs improved the entire school system:

School administrators became aware that one way in which to bring back the middle classes to the schools was to initiate special programs for the gifted. They therefore opened so-called "magnet schools" that offered enrichment activities in particular subject matter areas to interest sizable numbers of children who would have been studying elsewhere. The presence of the ablest began to make a difference in the total school atmosphere, which demonstrated that these children are capable of enhancing all education if their learning capacities are properly respected. (p. 40)

Gifted and talented programs have many generalizable traits that can benefit the mainstream of our educational system. Foremost are the traits we have discussed: quality, commitment, leadership, diversity of curriculum and instruction, and a whole-person approach. These traits are not educational outcomes; they are treatments or a form of unwritten instruction. These key elements are part of the process of gifted education and work to promote excellence in gifted programs. The similarities between model elements and conditions reported by MacArthur Fellows in the Richardson study are mutually reinforcing. As Cox, Daniel, and Boston (1985) report:

The inference of our look at the MacArthur Fellows is that the best of educational worlds should bring together supportive parents, imaginative teachers, and other good role models wherever they can be found at home, at school, or in the communities. If these personalities come together in a system that combines freedom with structure and rewards original thinking, even as it demands the best that every student can produce, then we can increase our chances of nurturing the inquiring, self-directed learners we all cherish. (p. 28)

These elements or conditions can be adapted to the mainstream educational system. The application of these elements to programs for dropouts has produced a significant improvement in personal and academic student behavior (see Fetterman 1981). Many gifted program features can be isolated and transmitted to new social contexts — including the regular school system— with some adaptation to the local environment. Moreover, these traits can become guiding principles in drawing the plans for new educational structures.

Revitalizing Gifted and Talented Education

Restoring gifted education will serve as a model of excellence for the restoration of the American educational system. A strengthened educational system can also become a symbol of quality, excellence, and commitment for nations throughout the world. Such a historical move would demonstrate that both the needs of the individual and the needs of society can be met in an egalitarian environment. Too many gifted and talented programs are gifted in name only. Many programs function only as a vehicle to secure state funding. Some programs have been allowed to decay, while others use confused definitions of giftedness and erratic identification practices (see Alvino, McDonnel, and Richert 1981). The Richardson study (Cox, Daniel, and Boston 1985) says the following: "From a national perspective the effort to improve education for our most capable students looks fragmented and discontinuous. There is no national consensus, not even a common pattern or a generally accepted approach to meeting the special needs of this population" (p. 42).

A National Center

Many steps can be taken to strengthen gifted programs. First, gifted education must become a federal priority. Increased federal support is vital. A major policy decision would reauthorize a national center for the gifted. The national Office of the Gifted and Talented (1972–1980) politicized issues of educating the gifted and talented and was accused of disseminating programs and models that represented the lowest educational common denominator. A new center with requisite controls and safeguards would ensure the promotion of strong empirical research and promulgate the "best education practices" throughout the nation. Controls would include the hiring of appropriate personnel, the selection of conscientious advisory panels and monitoring agencies, and the establishment of a sunset clause to build in a strong measure of academic and fiscal accountability.

In 1981, the Office of the Gifted and Talented in the Department of Education was eliminated. This move was largely a result of Zettel and Ballard's (1978) convincing argument for the dissolution of the office on behalf of the Council for Exceptional Children. Their goal was to provide the gifted child with a broader base of support by including the gifted child in the exceptional child category or concept. Their approach was logical given the politics of the period. However, they did not anticipate the rapidity with which the political climate would change and make this administrative association untenable. They also underestimated the significance of the symbolic role of the office, which focused national consciousness on the plight of gifted children. As a major consequence of the dissolution of the gifted office, "no federal moneys are directly earmarked for this upper 3 percent of the population. In our entire federal government, it appears that there is no office, section, or person charged with looking out after, providing information about, or coordinating efforts concerning our gifted and talented children" (Webb 1984, p. 8).

A national center would force us to consider the needs and potential of the gifted in planning the future of the United States. It could also facilitate the dissemination of useful information to parents, teachers, and administrators and provide grants for model programs. The center could promote existing exemplary programs, including the Olympics of the Mind (1983), the Future Problem Solving program (Crabbe 1982; Torrance and Torrance 1978; Torrance et al. 1978), and the American Mathematics Competitions (Mientka 1985), including the United States of America Mathematical Olympiad, the American Invitational Mathematics Examination, the American High School and Junior High School Mathematics Examination, the

International Baccalaureate (Cox and Daniel 1986; Kitano and Kirby 1986), and the Pyramid Project (Cox, Daniel, and Boston 1985).

A national center could also be a catalyst for much-needed research. New concepts and definitions of giftedness need to be explored. A qualitative leap is needed to shift from questions such as, How gifted is the child? to How is the child gifted? The cognitive processes of gifted children must be more clearly understood (see Karnes and Lee 1984; Hagen 1980; and Sternberg and Davidson 1983). An emphasis on the processes of thought is needed to refine gifted identification procedures. These insights would help balance our current overemphasis on statistical outcomes of intelligence tests. Research on the underachievers and culturally different could also receive needed attention. Moreover, a national center like the one in Israel could help to ameliorate much of the hostility toward gifted children that is endemic in the United States. The economic payback for this investment would be enormous.

The Gifted and Talented Children and Youth Education Act of 1985 is precisely the kind of step needed to establish a national center. The bill is designed ''to establish a Federal program to strengthen and improve the capability of State and local educational agencies and private nonprofit schools to identify gifted and talented youth with appropriate educational opportunities, and for other purposes'' (Biaggi et al. 1985). The bill asks Congress to find and declare that gifted and talented children are ''a national resource'' vital to ''the security and well being'' of the nation. In addition, it emphasizes that the potential of gifted children may be lost if it is not recognized and nourished during their elementary and secondary years of education. Moreover, the bill recognizes that economically disadvantaged gifted children ''are at greatest risk of being unrecognized'' and thus underserved. The bill suggests that the federal government is in the best position to stimulate appropriate research and provide technical assistance for many state and local educational agencies that are unable to provide appropriate programs for the gifted. The purpose of the Act is. . .

> to provide financial assistance to State and local educational agencies, institutions of higher education, and other public and private agencies and organizations, [and] to initiate a coordinating program of research, demonstration projects, personnel training, and similar activities designed to build a nationwide capability in our elementary and secondary schools to

identify and meet the special educational needs of gifted and talented children and youth. (Biaggi et al. 1985)

The bill recommends authorizing a $10 million appropriation for such a center. Although this amount is small given the scale of the project, it is sufficient to establish a viable national center. The funds will be for in-service training, establishment of model projects, and strengthening of ties between universities and local educational agencies to provide educational leadership for gifted programs, technical assistance, research, and evaluation. The proposed center would have as one of its highest priorities

> the identification of gifted and talented children and youth who may not be identified through traditional assessment methods (such as the limited English speaking, economically disadvantaged, handicapped, and women) and to education programs designed to include gifted and talented children and youth from such groups. (Biaggi et al. 1985, p. 7)

In addition, the center would be committed

> to programs and projects designed to develop or improve the capability of schools in an entire State or region of the Nation through cooperative efforts and participation of State and local educational agencies, institutions of higher education, and other public and private agencies and organizations (including business, industry, and labor), to plan, conduct, and improve programs for the identification and education of gifted and talented children and youth.

See also Jacob K. Javits's Gifted and Talented Children and Youth Education Act of 1987.

A National School

A national school for the gifted and talented would represent another major step forward. This school would be designed to help world class performers develop to their fullest potential in the arts and sciences. The school would be a federally funded residential high school located on the campus of a prominent university. Families would not be charged for their children's education beyond their local school tax. The number of students enrolled, the selection and admissions criteria, faculty recruitment, and curriculum development would be based on the same formula suggested for residential state high schools for mathematically talented youth (Stanley, in press). The only difference is that this would be a national school and serve a wider scope of gifted and talented students, ranging from scientists to poets. The standards for this school would be of the highest order. There would be, as Stanley recommends, minimum ability levels for any applicant — not norms. In addition, there "should be no place for patronage politics, preference for local teachers, and 'good ole boys' " in the recruitment of faculty (Stanley, in press). Such an environment would systematically group large numbers of the best achievers in the nation with their intellectual peers (see Zuckerman 1977). The school would serve to level out the egos of the best and brightest, and simultaneously help meet their special needs and help them make productive contributions to society. The school could be modeled after such exemplary schools as the Illinois Mathematics and Science Academy; the Louisiana School for Mathematics, Science, and the Arts; and the North Carolina School of Science and Mathematics.

The Next Step

Additional steps to improve gifted education include strengthening the links between universities and secondary schools with a focus on gifted programs. In addition to advanced placement, concurrent enrollment, and early entrance, talent searches and associated summer programs represent an important link between these institutions. A number of university-based summer programs for the gifted already exist throughout the country, but they must be expanded. In addition, more programs are needed.

The four major talent searches in the United States include Johns Hopkins's Study of Mathematically Precocious Youth (Stanley and Benbow 1982), Duke University's Talent Identification Program (see Sawyer 1982), Northwestern's Midwest Talent Search, and the University of Denver's Rocky Mountain Talent Search. (Arizona State University's Project for the Study of Academic Precocity is currently at Johns Hopkins.) Each of the universities has exemplary programs designed for verbally and mathematically gifted children. The programs allow gifted children to enroll in challenging courses. Johns Hopkins offers 2 three-week residential programs at Dickinson and Franklin and Marshall Colleges in Pennsylvania. Duke University offers 2 three-week sessions offering courses in chemistry, language, history, and various other subjects. Northwestern has an excellent reputation for its summer Cherubs program and the National High School Institute. The institute offers a six-day-a-week summer program for five weeks, covering the following subjects: journalism, radio, television, film, theater arts, music, engineering, and forensics. The University of Denver also offers a three-week summer institute for talent participants and a six-week program during the summer and the academic year — after school hours — for gifted children. Courses are provided for students at the preschool level through high school (see Katz and Seeley 1982).

Other universities also have excellent programs. The University of Northern Colorado offers gifted students a Summer Enrichment Program that consists of 4 seventy-minute classes lasting ten days. Day, evening, and weekend (research) activities are also available (see Betts 1982). Purdue offers a two-week residential leadership program called PALS (Purdue Academic Leadership Seminars) for high-achieving students in their junior year. It also provides a college credit program under the PALS umbrella for graduates of the program (see Feldhusen and Clinkenbeard 1982). The University of California, Berkeley, offers a Summer Program for Young Scholars that is designed for gifted and highly able students from ages seven through ten. The program focuses on the development of critical thinking, leadership skills, and familiarization with research methods (see UCB Gifted Program 1985). Indiana University provides summer residential programs for fifth- to ninth-grade gifted and talented students (see Spicker and Southern 1982). Mars Hill College in North Carolina provides a residential program for elementary and secondary students. The objectives of the program are to improve academic performance, creative expression, psychomotor development, and socialization skills (see Goodrum 1982). The University of Southern Mississippi offers a Summer Gifted Studies Program. It involves 3 two-week sessions emphasizing the improvement of cognitive, affective, and psychomotor abilities (see Karnes 1982). The University of Oregon offers a two-week Summer Enrichment Program for gifted and talented students (see Sheperd 1982). East Central Oklahoma State University also offers a summer lyceum for gifted and talented students. Students are provided instruction for three hours each morning for one week. The University of Wisconsin, Parkside (Kenosha, Wisconsin), offers a three-week College for Kids enrichment program for gifted children in kindergarten through fourth grade (see Robinson 1981). The Madison campus offers a three-week College for Kids enrichment program that focuses on critical thinking and creativity (see Clasen 1982). Approximately ten states have Governor's Honor's Programs or Governor's Schools for high-ability students. A number of summer programs for gifted and talented students also exist in the visual and performing arts. These programs go beyond entertainment and elementary enrichment: They contribute to the academic and psychological development of students. In addition, California State University, Sacramento; University of California, Irvine; the University of Washington; and Howard University have excellent models, programs, and projects.

Stanford University began a program to recruit students with strong mathematical talents — based on SAT examination performance — in 1985. Professors Rogosa, Efron, and Fetterman expanded the criteria in 1986 to emphasize such accomplishments as enrollment in gifted programs in elementary and high schools, the Rickover Institute (now the Research Science Institute), Bronx High School of Science, North Carolina School of Science and Mathematics, Stuyvesant High, the Ohio summer mathematics institute, Julian Stanley's mathematically precocious youth program (Stanley and Benbow 1982), and other notable programs, as well as participation in national and international chess and mathematical competitions, special projects, and winning such awards as the Westinghouse. In addition, we wrote to GATE coordinators in California urging them to interest gifted and talented students with strong mathematical talent in undergraduate study at Stanford. Plans are already in motion at Stanford to recruit nationwide gifted and talented students with an interest in computers, mathematics, the physical sciences, statistics, operations research, cryptography, information theory, and econometrics. Plans are also under way to expand the range of gifted children recruited (see Fetterman 1986b).

Stanford held its first gifted and talented education conference in 1986 to reestablish its role in the field, building on the early work of Terman. (See Terman 1925, 1954; Terman and Oden 1947, 1951, 1959; see also Sears and Barbee 1977.) One of the highlights of the conference was a session devoted to the Terman study. For the first time since the inception of Lewis Terman's landmark study of gifted individuals, four study participants emerged from their cloak of confidentiality and spoke to the gifted students at the conference. They shared their experiences in the study and as gifted individuals, linking the past with the present, inspiring the present generation with their accomplishments, and giving new life to the Terman study. Participant speakers included Robert Sears, professor emeritus of psychology and former dean of humanities and sciences at Stanford University; Robert Minge Brown, former president of the Stanford Board of Trustees and attorney in San Francisco; Juliana Gensley, professor of Education; and Eleanor Sully, actress and public health educator.

Endorsed by the California Association for the Gifted, the conference drew students, parents, directors, coordinators, and colleagues in the field. It was designed and hosted by Professor David Fetterman, School of Education at Stanford. Donald Kennedy, university president, welcomed participants. The conference's keynote speaker was Professor Julian Stanley from Johns Hopkins University, who discussed the study of mathematically precocious youth (SMPY) and highlighted his recent SMPY work in Taiwan and the People's Republic of China. In addition, Linda Forsyth, a leader in the California Gifted and Talented Education Program, and Sandra Kaplan, associate director of the National/State Leadership Training Institute on the Gifted and Talented, discussed recent trends in the field. Deans and faculty members from across the University discussed their research programs. Gifted students, educators, administrators, and parents participated in sessions ranging from lasers to adolescent initiation rites. (See Exhibit A for a detailed list of sessions and speakers and Exhibit B for the invitation and registration form.)

The conference had multiple purposes and many audiences. It provided a much-needed opportunity for cross-fertilization of ideas and experiences. One of its goals was to strengthen the ties between gifted and talented students and exceptional researchers. In the process, a stronger bond was forged between secondary and postsecondary institutions. The hope is that this conference will be a model for other universities across the United States. (See Walsh 1986; Shurkin 1986; Beyers 1986; O'Toole 1986; and Seawell 1986 for a more detailed description of the conference. See also Conference to Focus on Gifted, Talented Children 1986.)

We can also learn much from other nations, including our ideological competitors. The Soviet Union's impressive extracurricular educational system could easily be tailored to American cultural norms, vastly improving our general educational system (see Fetterman 1986b). Adopting some version of its after-school science and art programs would be responsive to Albert Shanker's call for alternative teaching styles and scoutlike after-school educational programs to supplement the conventional lecture format. Similarly, the flexibility of various countries about student transfers to appropriate facilities can be a useful object lesson for our often inflexible system of territorial (district-level) protectionism.

In addition, local, state, national, and international evaluations of these programs, such as the studies in this text, are necessary to monitor, refine, and improve gifted programs. As Alexander and Muia (1982) emphasize: "Evaluating is not the culmination of comprehensive and practical education for gifted learners, it is but the beginning of a revitalized program" (p. 287). The obstacles faced and the lessons learned from the gifted studies in this text provide generalizable guidelines for the entire educational system. A few of the most important findings and lessons drawn from these studies are as follows:

1. Standards of excellence must replace the mediocratic status quo.

2. Excellence and equal educational opportunity need not be mutually exclusive goals.

3. The development of a child's mind can not "survive educational neglect and apathy."

4. IQ tests, and other similar cognitive tests, do not equal intelligence. They measure a narrow spectrum of that psychological construct. These tests should be used for diagnosis and curriculum prescription. Moreover, they should not be used as the single most important criteria for identifying gifted children.

5. Student grouping should be guided by academic progress and potential, rather than by chronological age.

6. No ideal educational program applies to all types of students. Organizations do not exist in a cultural vacuum. An attempt should be made to match the values of a program with its community.

7. Acceleration is a useful educational tool for many students. It is time to break away from the age-in-grade, lock-step approach to education.

8. Peer reinforcement and close student-teacher relationships are instrumental tools in promoting high standards.

9. Political ties can either cement or undermine the stability of a program.

10. Quality, commitment, leadership, diversity of curriculum and instruction, and the whole-person approach are fundamental qualities of successful gifted and talented programs. Moreover, these features represent instrumental tools needed to revitalize our educational system.

A model of excellence can be crystallized from successful gifted and talented programs to facilitate a thorough and conscientious revision of our educational system. These reforms will be expensive, but they are essential if we are to overcome our wavering competitive edge in the global economy. As the National Commission on Excellence in Education concluded in its report (1982), we must accept this fact: "Excellence costs. But in the long run mediocrity costs far more" (p. 33).

The United States will begin to benefit from its rich natural resource only if it is willing to remove its cultural blinders toward gifted children. The myths, hostilities, and accusations of elitism that come from outside the program are rooted in a fundamental paradox inherent to the American cultural value system: the conflict between individualism and conformity (see Fetterman 1982, 1983, 1986a). This conflict, compounded by program isolation, has led detractors to equate equality of rights with equality of ability and achievement or results.

Internal hazards threaten these programs as well as external constraints. Self-imposed programmatic obstacles are gatekeepers that prevent gifted children from realizing their potential and subsequently their contribution to the future. An analysis of the day-to-day attitudes and activities of teachers and coordinators in the gifted programs provides a self-correcting mechanism by which to eliminate many of these internal disorders.

Fundamentally, however, "the great hostility toward precocious intellectual achievement that is endemic in this country" (Stanley and Benbow 1982) must come to an end. As long as we continue to view gifted programs as elitist rather than essential, we blind ourselves to the potential of the gifted child. Bigotry in any form clashes with democratic ideals. Typically, prejudice stems from ignorance, and it must be combated. Ignorance of the special needs of these children, and the role they can play in our future, can only be self-destructive in the long run — see the biography of William Sidis for a poignant example (Wallace 1986). Meritocracy and democracy need to be mutually compatible positions. As Brickman (1979) has argued:

> The dogma that democracy is at the opposite pole from meritocracy based on individual talent, skill, aptitude, ambition, and ability is at least open to serious difference of opinion. It is all too easy to dismiss the ideas of the world's greatest thinkers from ancient times to the present. A democratic society can pursue an egalitarian policy if it provides the fullest possible education for each person without regard to background and status, social, economic, political, religious, racial, sexual, physical, and mental. Under such a policy, all individuals will receive their democratic due, including those who are gifted and talented. (p. 329)

Exhibit A. *Detailed conference schedule.*

STANFORD UNIVERSITY CONFERENCE

ON

Gifted &
Talented Education

November 6-7, 1986

Thursday, November 6

1:00 - 1:30 Registration*

1:30 - 1:40 Introductory Remarks*

> *David Fetterman, Professor of Education, Stanford University*

1:40 - 2:00 Welcoming Remarks*

> *Donald Kennedy, President of Stanford*
> *Carolyn Lougee, Dean of Undergraduate Studies and Associate Dean of the School of Humanities and Sciences*

2:00 - 2:45 The Study of Mathematically Precocious Youth*

> *Julian Stanley, Professor of Psychology, Johns Hopkins University*

2:45 - 3:15 Break

3:15 - 4:05 Faculty/Student Speakers

Professor Anne Kiremidjian Civil Engineering	*Earthquakes: A Stanford Or A World Phenomenon?*	Bldg. 260, Room 276
Professor Tjeerd VanAndel Geology	*5,000 Years of Land Use and Abuse in Prehistoric Greece*	Bldg. 200, Room 34
Professor James Lowell Gibbs, Jr. Anthropology	*Anthropologists and Adolescent Initiation Rites*	Bldg. 200, Room 303
Professor Anthony E. Siegman Electrical Engineering	*Is There A Laser In Your Future?*	Bldg. 200, Room 305
Professor Charles Lyons Drama	*The Integration of Theory and Practice In the Single Artistic Imagination*	Bldg. 200, Room 02

4:15 - 5:05 Faculty/Student Speakers

Professor William Durham Anthropology	*On the Origin of Cultures: Turning Darwin Loose*	Bldg. 200, Room 02
Dr. Lisa Arkin and Dr. Susan Cashion Dance Division	*Dancing Through Time: Historical Overview of Ethnic Dance*	Bldg. 200, Room 34
Professor Patricia Jones Biological Sciences	*The Genetics of Immunity*	Bldg. 200, Room 303
Professor Nils Nilsson Computer Science	*Artificial Intelligence*	Bldg. 260, Room 276
Professor Channing Robertson Chemical Engineering	*Biotechnology--Opportunities at Stanford and After Stanford*	Bldg. 200, Room 305

5:30 - 6:30 Reception, Stanford Faculty Club, Red and Gold Lounges

6:30 - 8:00 Dinner, with performance by student music group, Stanford Faculty Club

> After dinner speaker:
>
> *Norman Wessells, Dean of Humanities and Sciences, Stanford University*

* Kresge Auditorium

Friday, November 7

8:45 - 9:00 Welcoming Remarks**

    Jean Fetter, Dean of Undergraduate Admissions

9:00 - 9:45 The Gifted in California**

    Linda Forsyth, Director of the California Gifted & Talented Education Program

9:45 - 10:00 Break

10:00 - 10:50 Faculty/Student Speakers

Professor Blas Cabrera Physics	*What Is the Dark Matter Around Our Galaxy?*	Bldg. 200, Room 203
Professor Sandra Richards Drama	*Theatre: A Window On the World*	Bldg.160, Room 161K
Professor Ronald Rebholz English	*Shakespeare's Plays in Relationship to Their Times*	Bldg. 200, Room 02
Professor Robert Osserman Mathematics	*Minimal Surfaces, Soap Bubbles and Computers*	Bldg. 200, Room 305

11:00 - 11:50 Faculty/Student Speakers

Professor William Reynolds Mechanical Engineering	*Interesting Views of Mechanical Engineering*	Bldg. 160, Room 161K
Dr. Carole Swain Director of the University of California, Berkeley, Summer Gifted Program	*Gifted and Talented Summer Programs*	Bldg. 200, Room 02
Professor Al Camarillo History	*Mexicans in California Society: Historical and Contemporary Perspectives*	Bldg. 200, Room 305
Professor David R. Rogosa School of Education	*Recruitment of Mathematical Talent*	Bldg. 200, Room 203

12:00 - 1:30 Lunch--Tresidder Oak East Lounge, Second Floor, Tresidder Student Union

    Luncheon presentation by James Gibbons, Dean of the School of Engineering, Stanford University

1:30 - 2:00 Leadership Training*

    Sandra Kaplan, Associate Director, National/State Leadership Training Institute on the Gifted and the Talented

2:00 - 2:45 Terman Study Group Returns to Stanford*

2:45 - 3:00 Closing Remarks*

    James Lyons, Dean of Student Affairs

3:00 - 4:00 Tours and free time on campus

The specific location for the tour you have selected will be available at registration.

    Acting, music, and dance demonstrations
    African and Afro-American Department videotape and presentation
    Campus tour highlighting points of interest
    Center for Computer Studies in Music tour
    Center for Integrated Systems tour
    Earth Sciences Labs
    Libraries tour
    SLAC tour
    SMPY Reunion (3:00 - 5:00)
    "Stanford Today," Undergraduate Admissions film and presentation
    The Stanford Museum, highlighting the Rodin Garden

* Kresge Auditorium
** Annenberg Auditorium

Exhibit B. Conference Program.

Stanford University's first Conference on Gifted and Talented Education will take place on November 6-7, 1986. Professor David Fetterman, distinguished researcher in gifted and talented education, will host the conference. University President Donald Kennedy will welcome participants. Professor Julian Stanley from Johns Hopkins University will be the keynote speaker, discussing The Study of Mathematically Precocious Youth. In addition, Dr. Linda Forsyth, Director, California Gifted and Talented Education Program, and Dr. Sandra Kaplan, Associate Director, National/State Leadership Training Institute on the Gifted and Talented, will discuss recent trends in the field.

Deans and faculty members from across the University will discuss their research programs. Campus tours will be arranged. Administrators from Stanford and other universities will also be available to discuss admission standards, financial aid, and other topics. Participants will have opportunities for informal exchange with speakers and faculty during meals and breaks. Students, parents, directors, coordinators, colleagues, and other parties interested in gifted and talented education are welcome. This conference is endorsed by the California Association for the Gifted.

The conference has multiple purposes and many audiences. It should provide a much needed opportunity for cross-fertilization of ideas and experiences. One goal of the conference is to strengthen the ties between gifted and talented students and exceptional researchers. In the process, a stronger bond will be forged between secondary and postsecondary institutions.

Please send registration materials and fees (if appropriate) to Dr. Michele Fisher, Director, The Center for Teaching and Learning, P.O. Box H, Stanford University, Stanford, California 94305.

ACCOMMODATIONS and **TRANSPORTATION**

Conference participants who will need to stay overnight on Thursday, November 6 are asked to make their own arrangements. To assist, we have enclosed a list of local hotels, their locations, and prices. For those of you flying in, we have also included information on transportation from either of the closest airports, San Francisco and San Jose, to the Stanford campus.

STANFORD
UNIVERSITY
CONFERENCE

*Gifted
&
Talented
Education*

THURSDAY AND FRIDAY
NOVEMBER 6 AND 7, 1986

FOR STUDENTS,
PARENTS,
DIRECTORS,
COORDINATORS,
COLLEAGUES,
AND
INTERESTED PARTIES

SCHEDULE

THURSDAY, NOVEMBER 6

1:00 - 1:30	Registration*
1:30 - 1:40	Introductory Remarks* **David Fetterman**, Professor of Education, Stanford University
1:40 -2:00	Welcoming Remarks* **Donald Kennedy**, President, Stanford University **Carolyn Lougee**, Dean of Under-graduate Studies and Associate Dean of the School of Humanities and Sciences, Stanford
2:00 - 2:45	The Study of Mathematically Precocious Youth* **Julian Stanley**, Professor of Psychology, Johns Hopkins University
2:45 - 3:15	Break
3:15 - 4:05	Faculty/Student Speakers Stanford faculty from the Humanities, Social Sciences, Sciences, and Engineering will speak on their areas of research. Several of them will be joined by their undergraduate research assistants. Speakers include: **Albert Camarillo**, History; **William Durham**, Anthropology; **Patricia Jones**, Biological Sciences; **Anne Kiremidjian**, Civil Engineering; **Charles Lyons**, Drama; **Nils Nilsson**, Computer Science; **Robert Osserman**, Mathematics; **William Reynolds**, Mechanical Engineering; **David Rogosa**, School of Education; **Channing Robertson**, Chemical Engineering; and **Ronald Rebholz**, English, among others.
4:15 - 5:05	Faculty/Student Speakers
5:30 - 6:30	Reception
6:30 - 8:00	Dinner, with performance by student music group After-Dinner Speaker: **Norman Wessells**, Dean of Humanities and Sciences, Stanford

FRIDAY, NOVEMBER 7

8:45 - 9:00	Welcoming Remarks** **Jean Fetter**, Dean of Under-graduate Admissions, Stanford
9:00 - 9:45	The Gifted in California** **Linda Forsyth**, Director of the California Gifted and Talented Education Program
9:45 - 10:00	Break
10:00 - 10:50	Faculty/Student Speakers
11:00 - 12:00	Faculty/Student Speakers
12:00 - 1:30	Lunch Lunch Speaker: **James Gibbons**, Dean of the School of Engineering, Stanford
1:30 - 2:00	Leadership Training* **Sandra Kaplan**, Associate Director of the National/State Leadership Training Institute on the Gifted and the Talented
2:00 - 2:45	Terman Study Group Returns to Stanford*
2:45 - 3:00	Closing Remarks
3:00 - 4:00	Tours and free time on campus Choose one: • Acting, music, and dance demonstrations • African and Afro-American Department videotape and presentation • Campus tour highlighting points of interest • Center for Computer Studies in Music tour • Center for Integrated Systems • Earth Sciences Labs • Libraries tour • Stanford Linear Accelerator Center tour • "Stanford Today," Undergraduate Admissions film and presentation • The Stanford Museum, highlighting the Rodin Garden • Walking tour of outdoor sculpture

*Kresge Auditorium
**Annenberg Auditorium

Bibliography

Academic Extension Branch. Education Department of Western Australia, 1984.

Adams, H. The British Association and Curriculum Enrichment in the County of Cleveland. *Gifted Education International*, 1985, 3(1):57–58.

Addison, L. Selection and Training of Teachers of the Gifted in the United States. *Gifted Education International*, 1983, 1(2): 60–64.

Alexander, P. Gifted Education: Needed Theory. *The Educational Forum*, 1984, 285–293.

Alexander, P., and Muia, J. *Gifted Education: A Comprehensive Roadmap.* Rockville, Maryland: Aspen Systems Corporation, 1982.

Allison, E. East Central University's Summer Lyceum for Gifted and Talented Students. *Journal for the Education of the Gifted*, 1982, 5(3):213–215.

Alvino, J., McDonnel, R.C., and Richert, S. National Survey of Identification Practices in Gifted and Talented Education. *Exceptional Children*, 1981, 48(2):124–132.

American Council on Education Business-Higher Education Forum. *America's Competitive Challenge: The Need for a National Response:* A Report to the President of the United States from the Business-Higher Education Forum: the Report in Brief. Washington, D.C.: The Forum 1983.

Applecross Senior High School. Intellectually Talented Students' Programme, Western Australia, 1983.

Archambault, F. Measurement and Evaluation Concerns in Evaluating Programs for the Gifted and Talented. *Journal for the Education of the Gifted*, 1984, 7(1):12–25.

151

Arnold, A. (ed.). Leadership: A Survey of Literature. In *A New Generation of Leadership*. Ventura, California: National/State Leadership Training Institute on the Gifted and Talented, 1977.

Australian Capital Territory. The Education of Gifted and Talented Children. *Schools Bulletin* 133, 1983.

Australian Department of Education and Youth Affairs. *Education in Australia*. Canberra: Australian Government Publishing Service, 1984, p. 22.

Avery, L., and Barolini, L. Survey of Provisions for Gifted Children in Illinois: A Summary Paper. *Journal for the Education of the Gifted*, 1979, 2(3):132–140.

Aylesworth, M. Guidelines for Selecting Instruments in Evaluating Programs for the Gifted. *Journal for the Education of the Gifted*, 1984, 7(1):38–44.

Baldwin, A. The Baldwin Identification Matrix. In *Educational Planning for the Gifted: Overcoming Cultural, Geographic, and Socioeconomic Barriers,* ed. A. Baldwin, G. Gear, and L. Lucito. Reston, Virginia: Council for Exceptional Children, 1978.

Ballard, B.J. Role of the Council for Exceptional Children in Federal Advocacy for the Gifted. *Journal for the Education of the Gifted*, 1984, 7(4): 238–243.

Baratz, J.C. Teaching Reading in a Urban Negro School System. In *Psychology of Education: New Looks,* ed., G.A. Davis and T.F. Waren. Lexington, Massachusetts: D.C. Heath, 1974.

Baratz, S.S., and Baratz, J.C. Early Childhood Intervention: The Social Science Base of Institutional Racism. *Harvard Educational Review,* 1970, 40:20–50.

Barbe, W.B. A Study of the Family Background of the Gifted. *Journal of Educational Psychology*, 1956, 47(5):302–309.

Barnette, J. Naturalistic Approaches to Gifted and Talented Program Evaluation. *Journal for the Education of the Gifted*, 1984, 7(1): 26–37.

The Basic Principles of the Unified Labour School. Moscow, Government Document, 1918.

Begle, E.G. Acceleration for Students Talented in Mathematics. Stanford, California: ED. 121607. Stanford University, Stanford Mathematics Study Group.

Bendix, R. Max Weber: An Intellectual Portrait. New York: Doubleday, 1965.

Bent, L.G., et al. *Grouping of the Gifted: An Experimental Approach.* Peoria, Illinois: Bradley University Publication, 1969.

Bereday, G.Z.F., Brickman, W.W., and Read, G.H. (eds.). *The Changing Soviet School.* Cambridge: The Riverside Press, 1960.

Berenzina, G.V., and Foteyeva, A.I. Educational Work and Extra-curricular Educational Establishments. In *Education in the USSR*, ed. N.P. Kugin et al., Moscow: Progress Publishers, 1972, p. 75.

Berk, R.A. Learning Disabilities as a Category of Underachievement. In *Learning-Disabled/Gifted Children*, ed. L.H. Fox, L. Brody, and D. Tobin. Baltimore, Maryland: University Park Press, 1983.

Berry, J.W. Temne and Eskimos' Perceptual Skills. *International Journal of Psychology*, 1966, 1:209–229.

Betts, G.T. A Step Forward for the Gifted: A Summer Enrichment Program. *Journal for the Education of the Gifted*, 1982, 5(3): 190–193.

Beyers, B. Job Openings Ahead: Consider Becoming a Professor. *Campus Report*, November 12, 1986, p. 13.

Biaggi, et al. Gifted and Talented Children and Youth Education Act of 1975. H.R. 3263. House of Representatives, 99th Congress, 1st Session, 1985.

Bishop, W.E. Successful Teachers of the Gifted. *Exceptional Children*, 1968, 317–324.

Bitan, D. Israel. In J. Gibson and P. Chennells, *Gifted Children: Looking to their Future.* London: Latimer New Dimensions Ltd., 1976, 322–327.

Bloom, B.S., et al. *Taxonomy of Educational Objectives:* Book 2, *Affective Domain.* New York: McKay, 1964.

Bloom, B.S., et al. *Taxonomy of Educational Objectives.* Handbook I, Cognitive Domain. New York: Longmans, Green and Co. 1956.

Borland, J. Teacher Identification of the Gifted: A New Look. *Journal for the Education of the Gifted*, 1978, 2(1):22–32.

Borthwick, B., et al. *The Gifted and Talented Students in Canada: Results of a Canadian Education Association Survey.* Canada: The Canadian Educational Association, 1980.

California State Department of Education. *Principles, Objectives, and Curricula for Programs in the Education of Gifted and Talented Pupils: Kindergarten through Grade Twelve.* Sacramento, California. California State Department of Education, 1979.

Callahan, C., and Caldwell, M. Using Evaluation Results to Improve Programs for the Gifted and Talented. *Journal for the Education of the Gifted,* 1984, 7(1):60-74.

Callow, R. The Schools Council Gifted Pupils Project. *Gifted Education International,* 1982, 1(1):49.

Canter, L., and Canter M. *Assertive Discipline: A Take Charge Approach.* Seal Beach, California: Canter and Associates, 1976.

Children's Palace. Moscow: Novosti Press, 1984.

Ciha, T., et al. Parents as Identifiers of Giftedness, Ignored but Accurate. *Gifted Child Quarterly,* 1974, 18:191-195.

Clark, B. *Growing Up Gifted: Developing the Potential of Children at Home and at School.* Columbus, Ohio: Charles E. Merrill Publishing Company, 1979.

_____*Growing Up Gifted: Developing the Potential of Children at Home and at School.* Second edition, Columbus, Ohio: Charles E. Merrill Publishing Company, 1983.

Clasen, D.R. Meeting the Rage to Know: College for Kids, an Innovative Enrichment Program for Gifted Elementary Children. Unpublished Reports, Department of Educational Psychology, University of Wisconsin, Madison, Wisconsin, 1982.

Clendening, C.P., and Davies, R.A. *Creating Programs for the Gifted: A Guide for Teachers, Librarians, and Students.* New York: R.R. Bowker Company, 1980.

_____. *Challenging the Gifted: Curriculum Enrichment and Acceleration Models.* New York: R.R. Bowker Company, 1983.

Coffey, K. Do You Really Believe in Gifted and Talented Education? Be an Advocate. *Journal for the Education of the Gifted,* 1984, 7(4): 278-285.

Colangelo, N. and R.T. Zaffrann (eds.). *New Voices in Counseling the Gifted.* Dubuque, Iowa: Kendall/Hunt Publishing Company, 1979.

Cole, M., Gay, J., Glick J., and Sharp, D.W. *The Cultural Content of Learning and Thinking: An Exploration in Experimental Anthropology.* New York: Basic Books, 1971.

Colon, P., and Treffinger D. Providing for the Gifted in the Regular Classroom. *Roeper Review*, 1980, 3:18–21.

Colton, D.L. *Policies of the Illinois Plan for Program Development for Gifted Children.* St. Louis, Mississippi: Center for Educational Field Studies, Washington University, August 1968.

Conference to Focus on Gifted, Talented Children. *Campus Report*, October 29, 1986, p. 4.

Cornish, R. Parents', Teachers' and Pupils' Perception of the Gifted Child's Ability. *Gifted Child Quarterly*, 1968, 34:14.

Cox, J. and Daniel, N. Options for the Secondary-Level G/T Student (Part II). *G/C/T*, 1983, 25:24–30.

Cox, J. Daniel, N., and Boston, B. *Educating Able Learners: Programs and Promising Practices.* Austin: University of Texas Press, 1985.

Crabbe, A.B. Creating a Brighter Future: An Update on the Future Problem Solving Problem. *Journal for the Education of the Gifted*, 1982, 5:2–9.

Cropley, A.J., et al. (eds.). *Giftedness: A Continuing Worldwide Challenge.* New York: Trillium, in press.

Cummings, W.K. *Education and Equality in Japan.* Princeton, New Jersey: Princeton University Press, 1980.

Davis, G.A., and Rimm, S.B. *Education of the Gifted and Talented.* Englewood Cliff, New Jersey: Prentice-Hall, Inc., 1985.

Day, P. *Center for Research on Social Organization.* Working Paper #99. Ann Arbor, Michigan: University of Michigan, 1974.

_____. Charismatic Leadership in the Small Organization. *Human Organization*, 1980, 39(1):50–58.

DeLeon, J. Cognitive Style Difference and the Underrepresentation of Mexican Americans in Programs for the Gifted. *Journal for the Education of the Gifted*, 1983, 6(3):167–177.

Department of Education. *A Review of the Core Curriculum for Schools.* Wellington: Government Printer, 1984.

Department of Education and Science. *Children and Their Primary Schools: A Report of the Central Advisory Council for Education.* Vol. I: *The Report.* London: Her Majesty's Stationery Office, 1967.

_____. *Gifted Children in Middle and Comprehensive Secondary Schools*. London: Her Majesty's Stationery Office, 1977.

Department of Education and Youth Affairs. *Education in Australia*. Canberra: Australian Government Publishing Service, 1984, p.22.

Department of Education and Science Library, *Select List of References on Sixth Form Colleges*. London: Department of Education and Science, 1975.

District's Gifted Program Charged with Discrimination. *Education Week*, August 22, 1984, pp. 3–4.

Dooley, R., et al. *The Report on the 1968 Summer Institute on Evaluation* (University of Illinois, July 29 – August 9, 1968). Champaign-Urbana. Cooperative Educational Research Laboratory, October 1968.

Dorset, D.I. The Field Dependence Hypothesis in Cross Cultural Perspective. *Dissertation Abstracts International*, 1970, 31 (6):3691–8.

Duncraig Senior High School. Information Guide for Parents, Western Australia, 1983.

Dunstan, J. *Paths to Excellence and the Soviet School*. Windsor, Great Britain: NFER Publishing Company, 1978.

The Educational System in the Federal Republic of Germany. Secretariat of the Standing Conference of Ministers of Education and Cultural Affairs of the Lander. Bonn: Courir-Druck, 1982.

Eisenberg, A., and George, W. Early Entrance to College: The Johns Hopkins Experience, *College and University*, 1979, 54(2):109–118.

Eisenstadt, S.N. *Selected Papers of Max Weber: On Charisma and Institution Building*. Chicago: University of Chicago Press, 1968.

Elwood, C. Acceleration of the Gifted. *Gifted Child Quarterly*, 1958, 2:21–23.

Feigenbaum, E.A., and McCorduck, P. *The Fifth Generation: Artificial Intelligence and Japan's Computer Challenge to the World*. New York: Signet, 1983.

Feldhusen, J.F. Programming for Gifted Students. Invited address, National Association for Gifted Children, Minneapolis, Minnesota, November, 1980.

Feldhusen, J.F., and Clinkenbeard, P.R. Summer Programs for the Gifted: Purdue's Residential Programs for High Achievers. *Journal for the Education of the Gifted*, 1982, 5(3):178–184.

Feldhusen, J.F., and Kolloff, M.B. A Three-Stage Model for Gifted Education. In *Programming for the Gifted, Talented, and Creative*, ed. R.E. Clasen, et al., Madison, Wisconsin: University of Wisconsin - Extension, 1981.

Fetterman, D.M. *Study of the Career Intern Program. Final Report: Program Dynamics: Structure, Function, and Interrelationships*. Mountain View, California. RMC Research Corporation, 1981.

_____. Gifted and Talented Programs: Special Privilege or Special Needs? Presented at the 81st Annual Meeting of the American Anthropological Association, Washington, D.C., December 1982.

_____. Margaret Mead, Gifted Children, and Ethnographic Educational Evaluation: A Case Study. Presented at the 82nd Annual Meeting of the American Anthropological Association, Chicago, Illinois, November 1983.

_____. *Ethnography in Educational Evaluation*. Beverly Hills, California: Sage Publications, 1984a.

_____. *Peoria Gifted Program Evaluation: Referral, Identification, and Selection*. Stanford, California: Stanford University, 1984b.

_____. Toward a Model of Excellence: Gifted Education. Presented at the Joint Meeting of the Evaluation Research Society and the Evaluation Network, San Francisco, California, October, 1984c.

_____. Gifted and Talented Education: A National Test Case in Peoria. *Educational Evaluation and Policy Analysis*, 1986a, 8(2):155–166.

_____. Recruiting the Mathematically Gifted at Stanford University, Presented at the California Association for the Gifted, Oakland, California, February 1986b.

_____. Gifted and Talented Education in the Soviet Union. *Gifted Education International*, 1987a, 4(3):180–183.

Fetterman, D.M. *Qualitative Approaches to Evaluation in Education: The Silent Scientific Revolution*. New York: Praeger Press, 1988.

_____. Gifted and Talented Education. In *Encyclopedia of School Administration and Supervision*, ed. R.A. Gorton. Phoenix, Arizona: The Oryx Press, in press.

Fetterman, D.M., and Pitman, M.A. *Educational Evaluation: Ethnography in Theory, Practice, and Politics.* Beverly Hills, California: Sage Publications, 1986.

Fetterman, D.M., and Wood, C.T. *Case Study Methodology for the Evaluation of the Gifted and Talented Education Program.* Mountain View, California: RMC Research Corporation, 1982.

Fichter, G. Ohio's Network: The Heart of it All. *Journal for the Education of the Gifted,* 1984, 7(4):291–296.

Foster, L. Building Materials for Gifted Children. *Gifted Education International,* 1983, 1(2):107–109.

Frasier, M. Counseling the Culturally Diverse Gifted. In *New Voices in Counseling the Gifted,* ed. N. Colangelo and R. Zaffrann. Dubuque, Iowa: Kendall/Hunt, 1979.

Freeman, J. The Gulbenkian Project on Gifted Children. In *Gifted Children: Looking to Their Future,* ed. J. Gibson and P. Chennells The National Association for Gifted Children. London: Latimer, 1976.

Gallagher, J.J. *Research Summary on Gifted Education,* Springfield, Illinois: State Department of Public Instruction, 1966.

————. *Teaching the Gifted Child.* Boston: Allyn and Bacon, Inc., 1985.

Gallup, G. The Gallop Poll Public Opinion 1983. Wilmington, Delaware: Scholarly Resources, Inc., 1984.

Gardner, J. *Excellence: Can We Be Excellent and Equal Too?* New York: Harper and Row, 1961.

GATE and the California Mentally Gifted Minor Program. Sacramento, California: California State Department of Education, 1978.

Getzels, J.W., and Dillon, J.T. The Nature of Giftedness and the Education of the Gifted. In *Second Handbook of Research on Teaching,* ed. R.M. Travers. Chicago: Rand McNally, 1973, 689–731.

Getzels, J.W., and Jackson, P.W. The Study of Giftedness: A Multidimensional Approach. In *The Gifted Student.* Washington, D.C.: Office of Education, U.S. Government Printing Office, 1960.

Gifted/Talented Children: Curriculum Ideas for Teachers. Toronto: Ontario Ministry of Education, 1978.

Glowka, D., *Schulreform und Gesellschaft in der Sowjetunion, 1958–1968: Die Differenzierung der Allgemeinbildenden Schule als Problem der Sowjetischen Bildungspolitik.* Stuttgart: Klett, 1970, p. 81.

Gogel, E.M. Gifted and Talented Advocacy Bibliography. *Journal for the Education of the Gifted*, 1984, 7(4):297–299.

Gold, M.J. *Education of the Intellectually Gifted.* Columbus, Ohio: Charles E. Merrill, 1965.

Goldberg, M.M. Recent Research on the Talented. *Teacher's College Record*, 1958, 60:150–163.

Goodlad, J.I. *A Place Called School: Prospects for the Future.* New York: McGraw-Hill Book Co., 1984.

Goodlad, J.I., and Anderson, R.H. *The Nongraded Elementary School.* New York: Harcourt Brace, 1959.

Goodrum, S. Summer Scholastics and Arts for the Gifted: A Holistic Approach. *Journal for the Education of the Gifted*, 1982, 5(3):170–173.

Gowan, J.C., and Demos, G.D *The Education and Guidance of the Ablest.* Springfield, Illinois, Charles D. Thomas, 1964.

Gray, W. Mentoring Gifted Talented Creative Students on an Initial Student Teaching Practicum: Guidelines and Benefits. *Gifted Education International*, 1984, 2(2):83–87.

Griffith, E.H. Response to Dr. Fetterman's Evaluation of the District #150's Gifted Program. Peoria: Peoria Public Schools, 1984a.

_____. In Hausser, M., Officials Study Peoria's Gifted Program Tests: Why Blacks, Other Minorities Seem to Have Trouble Getting Accepted. *Journal Star*, July 29, 1984b, p. D-4.

Guilford, J.P. *Fundamental Statistics in Psychology and Education.* New York: McGraw-Hill, 1956.

_____. Measurement and Creativity. *Theory into Practice*, 1966, 5:186–189.

_____. *The Nature of Human Intelligence.* New York: McGraw-Hill, 1967.

_____. *Creativity Tests for Children.* Orange, California: Sheridan Psychological Services, 1973.

_____. *Way Beyond the IQ.* Buffalo, New York: Creative Education Foundation, 1977.

Hagen, F. *Identification of the Gifted*. New York: Teachers College Press, 1980.

_____. Personal Communication, 1985.

Hans, N. The Evolution of Psychological Theories of Giftedness in the Soviet Union. In *The Yearbook of Education 1962: The Gifted Child*, ed. G.Z.F. Bereday and J.A. Lauwerys. London: Evans Brothers Ltd., 1962.

Hans, N. Washington School: Often Controversial and Misunderstood. *North Peoria Observer*, March 31, 1976, p. 5a.

Harmon, L.R. The Development of a Criterion of Scientific Competence. In *Scientific Creativity: Its Recognition and Development*, ed. C.W. Taylor and F. Barron. New York: John Wiley and Sons, 1963, 44–52.

Hausser, M. Stanford Consultant Impressed by Peoria's Gifted Program. *Journal Star*, September 18, 1984a, p. A-8.

_____. Gifted Program Bias Charged in Peoria Fund Cutoff. *Education Daily*, October 16, 1984b, p.8.

_____. School Board Discusses Gifted Program. *Journal Star*, November 6, 1984c, p. C-6.

Heller, K.A. *Formen der Hochbegabung Bei Kindern und Jugendlichen: Identifikation, Entwicklungsund Leistungsanalyse*. München: Universitat München, 1984.

_____. Identification and Guidance of Highly Gifted Children: Information About a Longitudinal Research Project. München: Universitat München, 1985.

Helson, R. Women Mathematicians and the Creative Personality. *Journal of Consulting and Clinical Psychology*, 1971, 36: 210–220.

Helson, R., and Crutchfield, R.S. Mathematicians: The Creative Researcher and the Average Ph.D. *Journal of Consulting and Clinical Psychology*, 1970, 34: 250–257.

Herche, P. Project Impact: Identification and Replication of Exemplary Gifted Programs in Illinois. *Journal for the Education of the Gifted*, 1979, 2(3):127–131.

Hill, C. New Zealand. In J. Gibson and P. Chennells, (eds.), *Gifted Children: Looking to Their Future*. London: Latimer New Dimensions Ltd., 1976, 343–348.

Hitchfield, E.M. *In Search of Promise: A Long-Term National Study of Able Children and Their Families*. London: Longman, 1973.

Hollingworth, T.S. *Children above 180 IQ*. New York: World Book, 1942.

Hoogh, H. The Individual Model for Fostering Giftedness. In *Giftedness: A Continuing Worldwide Challenge*, ed. A.J. Cropley et al. New York: Trillium, in press.

House, E.R., Kerins, C.T., and Steele, J. M. *The Demonstration Center: An Appraisal of the Illinois Experience*. Champaign-Urbana, Illinois: University of Illinois, December 1970.

_____. *The Gifted Classroom*. Champaign-Urbana, Illinois: CIRCE, June 1971a.

_____. *Educating the Talented: Illinois Gifted Program Final Evaluation Report*. Champaign-Urbana, Illinois: CIRCE, August 1971b.

House, E.R., Lapan, S., and Kerins, C.T. *A Preliminary Assessment of the Illinois Gifted Program*. Champaign-Urbana, Illinois: Cooperative Educational Research Laboratory, October 1968.

House, E.R., Steele, J.M., and Kerins, T. *The Development of Educational Programs: Advocacy in a Non-Rational System*. Champaign-Urbana, Illinois: CIRCE, November 1970.

House, E.R., et al. *The Visibility and Clarity of Demonstrations, and Appendices*. Champaign-Urbana, Illinois: Cooperative Educational Research Laboratory, May 1969.

Hoyle, E., and J. Wilks. *Gifted Children and Their Education*. London: Department of Education and Science, 1975.

Humphreys, L. In Hausser, M., Officials Study Peoria's Gifted Program Tests: Why Blacks, Other Minorities Seem to Have Trouble Getting Accepted. *Journal Star*, July 29, 1984, p. D-4.

Jacobs, J.C. Effectiveness of Teacher and Parent Identification of Gifted Children as a Function of School Levels. *Psychology in the Schools*, 1971, 8:140–142.

_____. Teacher Attitude toward Gifted Children. *Gifted Child Quarterly*, 1972, 16:23–26.

Jensen, A.R. *Educational Differences*. London: Methuen, 1973.

_____. *Bias in Mental Testing.* New York: The Free Press, 1980, 732-736.

Jones, M.A. Advocacy! Making a Difference for the Gifted. *Journal for the Education of the Gifted,* 1984, 7(4):270-277.

Justman, J. Academic Achievement of Intellectually Gifted Accelerants and Non-accelerants in Junior High School. *The School Review,* 1954, 62:142-150.

Karnes, F. Summer Residential Program for the Gifted: A University Model. *Journal for the Education of the Gifted,* 1982, 5(3):194-198.

Karnes, F., and Lee, L. Cognitive Abilities of Gifted Students as Measured by the Developing Cognitive Abilities Test. *Journal for the Education of the Gifted,* 1984, 7(3):170-177.

Karnes, M. In Hausser, M. Officials Study Peoria's Gifted Program Tests: Why Blacks, Other Minorities Seem to Have Trouble Getting Accepted. *Journal Star,* July 29, 1984, p. D-4.

Katz, E., and Seeley, K. The University of Denver's University for Youth. *Journal for the Education of the Gifted,* 1982 5(3):160-169.

Kelmscott Senior High School. Policy Statement for Intellectually Talented Students Group. Internal document, Western Australia 1983.

Kennedy, D. Helping Innovation: Advice for the Government That Didn't Ask. Presented at the San Diego Rotary Club, October 3, 1985.

Kerins, T., et al. *The Illinois Demonstration Centers—The Visitors' View.* Champaign-Urbana, Illinois: CIRCE, October 1969.

_____. *After the Visit: The Impact of Demonstration.* Champaign-Urbana, Illinois: CIRCE, May 1970.

Khatena, J. Some Problems in the Measurement of Creative Behavior. *Journal of Research and Development in Education,* 1971, 4(3):74-82.

Khatena, J. Creativity: Concept and Challenge. *The Educational Trends,* 1973, 8(1-4):7-18.

Khrushchev, N.S., in *Pravda*, September 21, 1958, as cited in W.W. Brickman, Educational Provisions for the Gifted and Talented in Other Countries, in the *Seventy-Eighth Yearbook of the National Society for the Study of Education: The Gifted and Talented — Their Education and Development*, Chicago: University of Chicago Press, 1979. Also as cited in N. DeWitt, *Education and Professional Employment in the USSR*, Washington, D.C.: U.S. Government Printing Office, 1961, p. 18.

King, H.R. The Comprehensive School in England: Broadening the Field of Opportunity and Stimulating Response. In *The Year Book of Education 1962: The Gifted Child*, eds. G.Z.F. Bereday and J.A. Lauwerys. London: Evan Brothers, 1962.

Kirst, M. Japanese Education: Its Implications for Economic Competition in the 1980s. *Phi Delta Kappan*, June 1981, 707–708.

Kitano, M.K. and Kirby, D.F. *Gifted Education: A Comprehensive View*. Boston: Little, Brown, & Company, 1986, p. 116.

Klausmeier, J. Effects of Accelerating Bright Older Elementary Pupils: A Follow-up. *Journal of Educational Psychology*, 1963, 54:165–171.

Koelle, W. Selection Procedures in the Schools of the Federal Republic of Germany. In *The Year Book of Education 1962: The Gifted Child*, eds. G.Z.F. Bereday and J.A. Lauwerys, London: Evans Brothers, 1962, 259–270.

Kohlberg, L., and Turiel, E. Moral Development and Moral Education. In *Psychology and Educational Practice*, ed. G. Lesser Chicago: Scott Foresman, 1971, 410–465.

Kozyr', B.I. Personal Communication, 1985.

Kreusler, A.A. *Contemporary Education and Moral Upbringing in the Soviet Union*. Ann Arbor, Michigan: University Microfilms International, 1976.

Krueger, M.L. *On Being Gifted*. American Association for Gifted Children. New York: Walker and Company, 1978.

Kulik, J.A., and Kulik, C.C. Effects of Accelerated Instruction on Students, *Review of Educational Research*, 1984, 54(3): 409–425.

Labov, W. Academic Ignorance and Black Intelligence, In *Psychology of Education: New Looks*, eds. G.A. Davis and T.F. Warren. Lexington, Massachusetts: D.C. Heath, 1974.

Laycock, S.R. Trends in the Education for the Gifted in Canada. In *The Year Book of Education 1962: The Gifted Child*, eds. G.Z.F. Bereday and J.A. Lauwerys. London: Evans Brothers, 1962.

Lemke, E. In Hausser, M. Officials Study Peoria's Gifted Program Tests: Why Blacks, Other Minorities Seem to Have Trouble Getting Accepted. *Journal Star*, July 29, 1984, p. D-4.

Lemov, P. That Kid Is Smart. *The Washingtonian*, 1979, 15(3):225–235.

Lett, W.R. Australia. The National Association for Gifted Children. In *Gifted Children: Looking to Their Future*, eds. J. Gibson and P. Chennells. London: Latimer, 1976, 285–288.

Levin, H.M. About Time for Educational Reform. *Educational Evaluation and Policy Analysis*, 1984, Summer, 6(2):151–163.

Lin, W. China Plans to End Soviet-Style Education System and Adopt Western Model. *The Chronicle of Higher Education*, June 26, 1985, pp. 1, 28.

McAlpine, D.M. *1984 Education of the Gifted and Talented*. Booklets 1–5. Palmerston North: Massey University (Education Department) Centre for Extramural Studies, 1984.

McAlpine, D.M., and McGrath, D.M. Gifted Children. In *Issues in New Zealand Special Education*, eds. S.J. Havill and D.R. Mitchell. Hodder and Stoughton, 1972.

McClelland, D.C. Testing for Competence Rather than for 'Intelligence.' *American Psychologist*, 1973, 28:1–14.

Maltby, F. Teacher Identification of Gifted Children in Primary Schools. In *Giftedness: A Continuing Worldwide Challenge*, ed. A.J. Cropley, et al. New York: Trillium, in press.

Marjoram, D.T.E. "Late Bloomers" — Provision for Able Youths and Adults in the United Kingdom. In *Giftedness: A Continuing Worldwide Challenge*, ed. A.J. Cropley, et al. New York: Trillium, in press.

Mead, M. The Gifted Child in the American Culture of Today. *Journal of Teacher Education*, 1954, 15(3):211–214.

166   EXCELLENCE AND EQUALITY

Meeker, M. *The Structure of Intellect: Its Interpretation and Uses.* Columbus, Ohio: Charles E. Merrill, 1969.

Merrifield, P.R., Gardner, S.F., and Cox, A.B. Aptitudes and Personality Measures Related to Creativity in Seventh Grade Children. *Report from the Psychological Laboratory*, No. 28. Los Angeles: The University of Southern California, 1964.

Mientka, W. American Mathematics Competition. Memorandum, 1985.

Mirman, N. Are Accelerated Students Socially Maladjusted? *Elementary School Journal*, 1962, 62:273–276.

Mitchel, P. (ed.). *A Policymaker's Guide to Issues in Gifted and Talented Education.* Alexandria, Virginia: National Association of State Boards of Education, 1981.

Mitchell, P.B. Mapping A State Advocacy Plan for the Gifted. *Journal for the Education of the Gifted*, 1984, 7(4):252–269.

Monsun, J.A. An Advocates' Guide to Advocating . . . or a Good Offense Without Being Offensive! *Journal for the Education of the Gifted*, 1984, 7(4):244–251.

Munday, L.A., and Davis, J.C. *Varieties of Accomplishment after College: Perspectives on the Meaning of Academic Talent.* Iowa City: American College Testing Program Research Report, No, 62, 1974.

National Commission on Excellence in Education. *A Nation at Risk.* Washington, D.C.: U.S. Department of Education, 1983.

New South Wales. *The Education of Children with Special Talents.* General Policy Statement. Sydney: Department of Education, New South Wales, 1983.

New System of Popular Education in U.S.S.R. Moscow: Academy of Pedagogical Sciences, 1960.

Newland, T.E. *The Gifted in Socioeducational Perspective.* Englewood, Cliffs, New Jersey: Prentice-Hall, Inc., 1976.

North Peoria Observer, Giving Gifted More is Millen's Daily Chore, by D. Grebner. November 17, 1982, p.10a.

O'Dell, F. Vocational Education in the USSR. In *Soviet Education in the 1980s*, ed. J.J. Tomiak. New York: St. Martin's Press, 1983.

Ogilvie, E. *Gifted Children in Primary Schools: The Report of Inquiry by Schools Council into the Teaching of Gifted Children of Primary Age. 1970-71.* London: Macmillan, 1973.

_____. The Schools Council Curriculum Enrichment Project. In *Educating the Gifted Child*, ed. R. Povey. London: Harper and Row, 1980.

Olympics of the Mind Association. *What is Olympics of the Mind?* Glassboro, New Jersey: OM Association, 1983.

Ontario Ministry of Education. *Gifted/Talented Children*, Curriculum Ideas for Teachers. Toronto: Ontario Ministry of Education, 1978, p.2.

O'Toole, K. Bright Adolescents Take College Tests, Tailored Courses. *Campus Report*, November 12, 1986, p. 11.

Painter, F. Research into Attainment Levels of Gifted British Primary School Children, In *Gifted Children: Looking to Their Future*, eds. J. Gibson and P. Chennells. The National Association for Gifted Children. London: Latimer, 1976.

Parkyn, G.W. *Children of High Intelligence: A New Zealand Study.* Wellington: New Zealand Council for Educational Research, 1948.

_____. *Children of High Intelligence: A New Zealand Study.* Wellington: New Zealand Council for Educational Research. 1953.

_____. The Mental Health of the Gifted Child. In *Mental Health and the Community*, ed. P.J. Lawrence. Christchurch, New Zealand: Canterbury Mental Health Council, 1963.

_____. The Identification and Evaluation of Gifted Children: A New Perspective. In *Gifted Children: Looking to Their Future*, eds. J. Gibson and P. Chennells. The National Association for Gifted Children. London: Latimer, 1976..

_____. Gifted Children: Understanding Their Feelings, The Wellspring of Creative Art. In *Education Reality, and the Gifted Child*. The Third National Conference on Gifted and Talented Children. New Zealand: Christchurch, 1984.

Passow, A.H. *Reforming Schools in the 1980s: A Critical Review of the National Reports.* New York: ERIC Clearinghouse on Urban Education, 1984.

Pegnato, C.W., and Birch, J.W. Locating Gifted Children in Junior High Schools: A Comparison of Methods. *Exceptional Children*, 1959, 25:300-304.

Plowman, P.D. Programming for the Gifted Child. *Exceptional Children*, 1969, 547–551.

Pole, J.R. *The Pursuit of Equality in American History.* Berkeley: University of California Press, 1978.

Postlethwaite, K., and Denton, C. Identifying More Able Pupils in Secondary Schools. *Gifted Education International*, 1983, 1(2):92–96.

Pringle, M.L.K. *Able Misfits: A Study of Education and Behavior Problems of 103 Very Intelligent Children, IQ 120–200.* London: Longman, 1970.

Print, M. Curriculum Materials for Able Children. *Gifted Education International*, 1983, 1(2):103–106.

Project Equity. Ottawa: Carleton Board of Education, 1973.

Public Schools Commission Second Report, Vol. I: *Report on Independent Day Schools and Direct-Grant Grammar Schools.* London: Her Majesty's Stationery Office, 1970.

Queensland, *Education of the Gifted in Queensland State Schools.* Brisbane: Queensland Department of Education, 1983.

Reid, N. A Differentiated Curriculum for Gifted Children: A New Zealand Perspective. In *Education, Reality, and the Gifted Child.* The Third National Conference on Gifted and Talented Children. New Zealand: Christchurch, 1984.

Renzulli, J.S. *A Guidebook for Evaluating Programs for Gifted and Talented.* Ventura, California: Office of the Ventura County Superintendent of Schools, 1975.

————. *The Enrichment Triad Model.* Wethersfield, Connecticut: Creative Learning Press, 1977.

————. Identifying Key Features in Programs for the Gifted. In *Gifted and Talented Education in Perspective*, eds. J. Renzulli and E. Stoddard. ERIC Clearinghouse on Handicapped and Gifted Children. Reston, Virginia: The Council for Exceptional Children, 1980.

————. Dear Mr. Copernicus: We Regret to Inform You . . . *Gifted Child Quarterly*, Winter 1982, 26(1):11–14.

————. Evaluating Programs for the Gifted: Four Questions about the Larger Issues. *Gifted Education International*, 1984, 2(2):83–87.

Renzulli, J.S., and Hartman, R.K. Scale for Rating Behavioral Characteristics of Superior Students. *Exceptional Children*, 1971, 38(3):243-248.

Renzulli, J., Smith, L., and Reis, S. *The Revolving Door Identification Model*. Mansfield Center, Connecticut: Creative Learning Press, 1981.

————. Curriculum Compacting: An Essential Strategy for Working with Gifted Students. *Gifted Education International*, 1983, 1(2):97-102.

Reynolds, C.R., and Jensen, A.R. WISC-R Subscale Patterns of Abilities of Black and White Matched on Full Scale IQ. *Journal of Educational Psychology*, 1983, 75(2):207-214.

Reynolds, M., Birch, J., and Tuseth, A. Research on Early Admissions. In W. Dennis & M. Dennis (eds.), *The Intellectually gifted: An Overview*. New York; Grune and Stratton, 1976.

Rimm, S.B., and Davis, G.A. Five Years of International Research with GIFT: An Instrument for the Identification of Creativity. *Journal of Creative Behavior*, 1980, 14:35-46.

————. Identifying Creativity. Part II. *G/C/T*, 1983:19-23.

Ripple, R. A Controlled Experiment in Acceleration from the Second to the Fourth Grade. *Gifted Child Quarterly*, 1961, 5:119-120.

Rimm, S., Davis, G. and Bien, Y. Identifying Creativity: A Characteristics Approach. *Gifted Child Quarterly*, 1982, 26(4): 165-71.

Robinson, B. College for Kids: The Anatomy of a Summer Enrichment Program for K-4 Gifted Children at the University of Wisconsin-Parkside. In *Programming for the Gifted, Talented, and Creative: Models and Methods*, ed. R.E. Clasen, et al. Madison, Wisconsin: University of Wisconsin - Extension, 1981.

Roeper, G.A. Education of the Gifted. In *The Changing Soviet School*, eds. G.Z.F. Bereday, W.W. Brickman, and G.H. Read. Boston: Houghton Mifflin, 1960, 360-378.

Rohlen, T.P. *Japan's High Schools*. Berkeley, California: University of California Press, 1983.

Roldan, A. Report on a Survey of Gifted Education Based on the Fifth World Conference in Manila. In *Giftedness: A Continuing Worldwide Challenge*, ed. A.J. Cropley. New York: Trillium, in press.

Sawyer, R.N. The Duke University Program to Identify and Educate Brilliant Young Students. *Journal for the Education of the Gifted*, 1982, 5(3)185–189.

Schab, F. Deceit among the Gifted. *Journal for the Education of the Gifted*, 1980, 3(3)129–132.

Schairer, R. The German Institute of Talent Study in Cologne. In *The Year Book of Education 1962: The Gifted Child*, eds. G.Z.F Bereday and J.A. Laurwerys. London: Evans Brothers, 1962, 271–274.

School Officials, Gill Plan Caucus to Avoid Lawsuit. *Journal Star*, October 19, 1984, p. A-5.

Schultze, W., and Fuhr, C. Federal Republic of Germany. In *Schools in Europe*, ed. W. Schultze. Weinheim: Beltz, 1968, 494.

————. *Das Schulwesen in der Bundesrepublik Deutschland.* Weinheim: Beltz, 1973, 83–90.

Sears, P., and Barbee, A. Career and Life Satisfaction among Terman's Gifted Women. In *The Gifted and the Creative: A Fifty-Year Perspective*, ed. C.H. Solano. Baltimore: The Johns Hopkins University Press, 1977.

Seawell, M.A. Universities Advised to Nurture and Cherish Math Prodigies. *Campus Report*, November 12, 1986, p. 11.

Sellin, D.F. and Jack W. Birch. *Educating Gifted and Talented Learners*. Rockville, Maryland, Aspen Systems Corp. 1980.

Services for Children: Children with Special Talents. Sydney: New South Wales Department of Education, 1983.

Shade, B. Sociopsychological Characteristics of Achieving Black Children. In *Simple Gifts*, eds. R. Clasen and B. Robinson. Madison, Wisconsin. University of Wisconsin - Extension, 1978, 229–242.

Sheperd, G. Learning Not to Be Afraid to Be Smart: University of Oregon's Summer Enrichment Program for Talented and Gifted Students. *Journal for the Education of the Gifted*, 1982, 5(3):199–203.

Shields, J.B. *The Gifted Child.* Slough, Bucks: National Foundation for Educational Research in England and Wales, 1968.

Shurkin, J. State Official: Special Programs for Gifted Not "Elitist." *Campus Report*, November 12, 1986, p. 12.

Singleton, J. *Nichu: A Japanese School.* New York: Holt, Rinehart, and Winston, 1967.

Sjogren, D., et al. *Training Materials for Gifted Evaluation Institute* (University of Illinois, July 29–August 9, 1968). Champaign-Urbana, Illinois: CIRCE, August 1968.

South Australia. Policy Regarding Fostering Special Gifts and Talents among Children. *Education Gazette*, South Australia, 1983, 23(11).

Spicker, H., and Southern, W. Indiana University's College for Gifted and Talented Youth. *Journal for the Education of the Gifted*, 1982, 5(3):155–159.

Stanley, J.C. On Educating the Gifted. *Educational Researcher*, March 1980, 8–12.

————. Residential State High Schools for Mathematically Talented Youths? A Qualified "Yes." *Phi Delta Kappan*, in press.

Stanley, J.C., and Benbow, C.P. Educating Mathematically Precocious Youths: Twelve Policy Recommendations. *Educational Researcher*, May 1982, 4–9.

Stedman, L.C., and Smith, M.S. Recent Reform Proposals for American Education. Manuscript to be published in *Contemporary Education Review.* Madison, Wisconsin: Wisconsin Center for Education Research, 1983.

Steele, J.M. *Dimensions of the Class Activities Questionnaire.* Champaign-Urbana, Illinois: CIRCE, October 1969.

Steele, J.M., et al. *Instructional Climate in Illinois Gifted Classes.* Champaign-Urbana, Illinois: CIRCE, August 1970.

————. Cognitive and Affective Patterns of Emphasis in Gifted and Average Illinois Classes. *Exceptional Children*, 1971, 37(10):757–759.

Sternberg, R.J., and Davidson, J.E. Insight in the Gifted. *Educational Psychologist*, 1983, 18(1):51–57.

Stogdill, R. *Handbook of Leadership: A Survey of Theory and Research.* New York: The Free Press, 1974.

Stone, R. Manchester Grammar School. In *British Secondary Education: Overview and Appraisal*, ed. R.E. Gross. London: Oxford University Press, 1965.

Swanbourne Senior High School. Intellectually Talented Students Programme, Western Australia, 1984.

Swerdlik, M. In Hausser, M. Officials Study Peoria's Gifted Program Tests: Why Blacks, Other Minorities Seem to Have Trouble Getting Accepted. *Journal Star*, July 29, 1984, p. D-4.

Switzer, C., and M.L. Nourse. Reading Instruction for the Gifted Child in First Grade. *Gifted Child Quarterly*, 1979, 23:323–331.

Syphers, D. *Gifted and Talented Children: Practical Programming for Teachers and Principals*. Arlington, Virginia: The Council for Exceptional Children, 1972.

Tannenbaum, A.J. *Gifted Children: Psychological and Educational Perspectives*. New York: Macmillan, 1983.

Tan-Willman, C., and Gutteridge, D. Creative Thinking and Moral Reasoning of Academically Gifted Secondary School Adolescents. *Gifted Child Quarterly*, Fall 1981, 25(4):149–153.

Tasmania. *Gifted Talented Students in Schools*. Hobart: Education Department, Tasmania, 1984.

Taylor, C.W. How Many Types of Giftedness Can Your Program Tolerate? *Journal of Creative Behavior*, 1978, 12:39–51.

Taylor, P.H., Reid, W.A., and Holley, B.J. *The English Sixth Form: A Case Study in Curriculum Research*. London: Routledge and Kegan Paul, 1974.

Taylor, R. The gifted and talented. Taped lecture on gifted and talented education, 1980. Englewood, Colorado: Educational Consulting Associates.

Terman, L.M. and Oden, M.H. *The Gifted Child Grows Up*. California: Stanford University Press, 1947.

Terman, L.M. and Oden, M.H. *Genetic Studies of Genius*. Vol. 4: *The Gifted Child Grows Up*. Stanford, California: Stanford University Press, 1951.

————. The Discovery and Encouragement of Exceptional Talent *American Psychologist*, 1954, 9:224.

————. *The Gifted Group at Mid-Life: Thirty-Five Years' Follow-up of the Superior Child*. Stanford, California: Stanford University Press, 1959.

Terman, L.M., et al. *Genetic Studies of Genius*, Vol. 1: *Mental and Physical Traits of a Thousand Gifted Children.* Stanford University Press, 1925.

Tasmania. *Gifted and Talented Students in Schools.* Hobart: Education Department, Tasmania, 1984.

Thomas, A., Maesydderwen Comprehensive school (Breconhire). In *British Secondary Education*, ed. R.E. Gross. London: Oxford University Press, 1965.

Tocqueville, Alexis de. *Democracy in America.* Translated by Henry Reeve. Vol. I (pp. 1–417). New York: The Colonial Press, 1899.

Tocqueville, Alexis de. *Democracy in America.* Translated by Henry Reeve. Vol. II (pp. 419–868). New York: D. Appleton and Company, 1899.

Torrance, E.P. *Torrance Tests of Creative Thinking.* Lexington, Massachusetts: Personnel Press, 1966.

_____. *Torrance Tests of Creative Thinking: Norms-Technical Manual.* Lexington, Massachusetts: Personnel Press, 1974.

_____. Lessons about Giftedness and Creativity from a Nation of 115 Million Overachievers. *Gifted Child Quarterly*, 1980, 24(1):10–14.

Torrance, E.P., Khatena, J., and Cunnington, B.F. *Thinking Creativity with Sounds and Words.* Lexington, Massachusetts: Personnel Press, 1973.

Torrance, E.P., Torrance, J.P. The 1977–78 Future Problem-solving Program: Interscholastic Competition and Curriculum Project. *Journal of Creative Behavior*, 1978, 12:87–89.

Torrance, E.P., et al. *Handbook for Training Future Problem-solving Teams.* Athens, Georgia: Georgia Studies of Creative Behavior, University of Georgia, 1978.

Treffinger, D.J. Teaching for Self-Directed Learning: A Priority of the Gifted and Talented. *Gifted Child Quarterly*, 1975, 19:46–59.

_____. The Progress and Peril of Identifying Creative Talent among Gifted and Talented Students. *Journal of Creative Behavior*, 1980, 14 (1):20–34.

_____. *Blending Gifted Education with the Total School Program.* Williamsville, New York: Center for Creative Learning, 1981.

_____. Myth: We Need to Have the Same Scores for Everyone! *Gifted Child Quarterly*, Winter 1982, 26(1):20-21.

Treffinger, D.J., and Poggio, J.P. Needed Research on the Measurement of Creativity. *Journal of Creative Behavior*, 1972, 6 (4):253-267.

Treffinger, D.J., Renzulli, J.S., and Feldhusen, J.F. Problems in the Assessment of Creative Thinking. *Journal of Creative Behavior*, 1971, 5(2):104-112.

Tuttle, F.B., Jr. *Gifted and Talented Students*. Washington, D.C.: National Education Association, 1978.

Tuttle, F.B., Jr., and Becker, L.A. *Characteristics and Identification of the Gifted and Talented Students*. Washington, D.C.: National Educational Association, 1980.

The UCB Gifted Program *A Summer Program for Young Scholars*. Berkeley, California: Graduate School of Education. Brochure, 1985.

U.S. Commissioner of Education, S.P. Marland, Jr. *Education of the Gifted and Talented*. Department of Health, Education, and Welfare, August 1971.

U.S. Department of Commerce. *1980 Census of Population and Housing: Census Tracts - Peoria, Illinois*. Washington, D.C.: Bureau of the Census, 1980 (Issued August 1983).

U.S. Public Health Service Report. Washington, D.C.: Government Documents, 1912.

Vare, J. Moral Education for the Gifted: A Confluent Model. *The Gifted Child Quarterly*, Fall 1979, 23(3):487-499.

Vernon, P.E. *Intelligence and Cultural Environment*. London: Methuen, 1969.

Vogel, E.F. *Japan as Number One: Lessons for America*. New York: Harper and Row, 1979, 158-183.

Vogeli, B.R. *Soviet Secondary Schools for the Mathematically Talented*. Washington, D.C.: National Council of Teachers of Mathematics, 1968, p. 11.

Wagner, H., and Zimmermann, B. Identification and Fostering of Mathematically Gifted Students. In *Giftedness: A Continuing Worldwide Challenge*, eds. A.J. Cropley, et al. New York: Trillium, in press.

Walker, J.J. Developing Values in Gifted Children. *Teaching Exceptional Children*, 1975, 7(3):98–100.

Wallace, A. *The Prodigy: A Biography of William James Sidis.* New York: E.P. Dutton, 1986.

Wallace, B. An Examination of the Development of the Concept of Gifted Education in the United Kingdom; An Analysis of the Current Position with Suggestions for the Positive Way Forward. *Gifted Education International*, 1985, 3(1):4–11.

Wallach, M.A. Creativity. In *Carmichael's Manual of Child Psychology*, ed. P.H. Mussem. New York: John Wiley, 1970.

Wallach, M.A., and Kogan, N. *Modes of Thinking in Young Children.* Lexington, Massachusetts: Personnel Press, 1966.

Walsh, E. "Gifted Kids" of Yesteryear Return to Campus. *Campus Report*, November 12, 1986, 12–13.

Wasson F.R. Advocacy for Gifted and Talented in Florida: Why It Works. *Journal for the Education of the Gifted*, 1984, 7(4): 286–290.

Webb, J.T. Problems of the Gifted Get Too Little Notice, Psychologists Says (quoted in interview by Cheryl Fields) *Chronicle for Higher Education*, 1984, 29(2):1, 8.

Weber, M. *Economy and Society: An Outline of Interpretive Sociology.* (G. Roth and C. Wittich, eds.) New York: Bedminister Press, 1968.

Wechsler, D. *Manual for the Wechsler Intelligence Scale for Children Revised.* New York: The Psychological Corporation, 1974.

Western Australia. Gifted and Talented Children in Western Australian Schools. Policy from the Director-General's Office, No. 15. Education Department of Western Australia, 1978.

Whitmore, J.R. *Giftedness, Conflict, and Underachievement.* Boston: Allyn and Bacon, 1980.

_____. TAG's Central Mission: Advocacy. *Journal for the Education of the Gifted*, 7(4):227–228.

Williams, F.E. *Classroom Ideas for Encouraging Thinking and Feeling.* Buffalo, New York: DOK Publishers, 1970.

Winterbourn, R. Identification of the Gifted in a Largely Egalitarian Society (New Zealand). In *The Yearbook of Education 1962: The Gifted Child*, eds. G.Z.F. Bereday and J.A. Lauwerys. London: Evans Brothers, 1962, 236–245.

Witkins, H.A. Socialization, Culture, and Ecology in the Development of Group and Sex Differences in Cognitive Style, *Human Development*, 1979, 22:358–372.

Witkin, H.A., et al. *Psychological Differentiation*. New York: Wiley Press, 1974.

Wood, C.T. Policy Analysis of California's Program for Gifted and Talented Students. *Educational Evaluation and Policy Analysis*, 1985, 7(3):281–287.

Wood, C.T., and Fetterman, D.M. *Study Design for the Evaluation of the Gifted and Talented Pupil Program*. Mountain View, California: RMC Research Corporation, 1981a.

————. *First Annual Report of the Evaluation of the Gifted and Talented Education Program*. Mountain View, California: RMC Research Corporation, 1981b.

————. *Final Report of the Evaluation of the Gifted and Talented Education Program*. Mountian View, California: RMC Research Corporation, 1983.

Zaffrann, R. Gifted and Talented Students: Implications for School Counselors, *Roeper Review*, 1978, 1:9–12.

Zettel, J.J., and Ballard, J. A Need for Increased Federal Effort for the Gifted and Talented. *Exceptional Children*, 1978, 261–267.

Zha, Z. A Study of the Mental Development of Supernormal Children in China. In *Giftedness: A Continuing Worldwide Challenge*, eds. A.J. Cropley, et al. New York: Trillium, in press.

Zuckerman, H. *Scientific Elite: Nobel Laureates in the United States*. New York: The Free Press, 1977.

Author Index

Subject Index

Good Morning, America show 80
Governor's Honor's Program 141
Governor's Schools 141
grading 17, 52, 55, 67–72
grouping structures 16, 29–39, 95–123, 143; acceleration 16, 37–38, 106, 116, 117, 122; cluster grouping 16, 17, 34–36, 43–46, 47; enrichment 16, 36, 73–94, 99–102, 103, 104, 112–113, 116–117, 118–120, 122; independent study 16, 36–37, 117; part-time (see pull-out and seminar); pull-out groups 16, 34, 41–43, 112, 117, 122; postsecondary opportunities 16, 38–39, 139–142; special day classes 16, 31–33, 73–94, 105, 117
Guilford, J. 29, 30, 63

Haertel, Edward 109
Hagen, F. 109
Harvard 66
Harvard's Institute for Principals 5
Havana Hopewell Indians (archaeological dig) 76–77
Hawiian pidgin 60
Heller, Kurt 109, 122
Henmon-Nelson Test of Mental Ability 27
high achievers 35, 84, 91
Hiroshima 54
Hispacis 58–59
historical materialism 97
holography 46
hostility 1, 8, 18, 19, 31–33, 39, 45, 51–52, 56, 66, 79, 81, 137, 144; attitude and associations 48, 64–65, 144
Howard University 141

identification 16, 25–29, 39, 59–62, 73–94, 95–123; committee review 29, 82–88, 93; creative 16, 17, 26, 29, 61; documentation 27, 28; growth-scale values 87; high achievement 16, 25, 28, 73–94; intellectual ability 16, 25, 27–28, 73–94; leadership 16, 26, 29; normal curve equivalents 87; percentiles 86–87; raw scores 86–87; screen-

ing 27, 82–88; searching 27, 82–88; specific academic 16, 26, 28; standard age scores 86; visual and performing arts 16, 26, 29; weighting system 86–87
Illinois 73
Illinois Mathematics and Science Academy 139
Illinois State Board of Education 74, 82, 90; evaluations of gifted programs 74; Office of the Superintendent of Public Instruction 83, 93
independent study 16, 36–37, 95–123
Indiana University 140
individualism xiii, 2, 4, 9, 11, 144
insightful thinking 63, 137
Institute of Chemical Physics (U.S.S.R.) 101
Institute of Organic Chemistry (U.S.S.R.) 101
Institute of Space Studies (U.S.S.R.) 100
instruction xv, 19, 41–56, 65–72, 74–82, 95–123. See also grouping structures and model of excellence
international 18, 95–123
International Baccalaureate 137
intracultural diversity 95
isolation 33, 48–49, 53, 56, 119, 144
Israel 18, 118–120, 121, 122–123, 137; curriculum 120; Department for Gifted Children 118–119, 122; egalitarian 118; enrichment 118–120, 123; Ministry of Education and Culture 118, 122; Ofek School in Jerusalem 119; Programs 119–120; special classes 119–120, 122; Weizmann Institute 119–120; Welfare Programs and Renewal Projects Department 119
Italian immigrants 61
IQ 3, 17, 57, 59–62, 89, 91, 94, 115, 119, 143

Japan 18, 120–121, 123; cars 126; electronics 126; entrance examinations 120–121; Japanese Ministry of International Trade and Industry 126; microelectronic chip 126

odarennye deti (U.S.S.R. gifted children) 97
Office of the Gifted and Talented in the Department of Education 136
Ohio State University summer mathematics institute 141
Olympics of the Mind 136
optical scoring 85
Ortar test 119

parents 7, 10, 52, 53, 65–70, 80–82, 110, 130, 135
Paris 75
Parkyn, G. 107
Pasadena Association of Gifted Education 22
Passow, A. 109
Peabody Individualized Achievement Test 28
Peabody Picture Vocabulary Test 27
peer pressure 49, 65–72, 131, 143
pencils 85
People's Republic of China 142
Peoria 17, 73–94
Peoria Public School's Academically Gifted Program 74; administration 77; climate 78–82; court 94; curriculum 74–82; enrollment 91; evaluation 76, 82–94; fiscal issues 73; identification procedures 84–88; in-service training 84, 93; media, 92–94; parents 80–82; program 74–82; referral mechanisms 82–84; replacement slots 87–88, 93; selection committee 85, 93; teachers 77–82, 83
perfectionist syndrome 66
Philippines 121; College of Education 121; National School of Arts 121; Philippine Science High School 121; Silahis Center 121
policy recommendations xv, 125–145
Polish immigrants 61
politics xiii, xv, 1–7, 16, 43–45, 57, 59, 64–65, 74, 88, 127, 131, 132, 143
postsecondary opportunities 16, 38–39, 139–142
Princeton 66

Project for the Academically Talented of the National Association 116
psychological pressure 17, 52, 65–67
pull-out groups 16, 34, 41–43, 112, 117, 122
Purdue University 109, 140; Purdue Academic Leadership Seminars 140
Pyramid Project 137

quality xv, 19, 32, 128–130, 144
qualitatively different xiv, 32, 35, 36, 41–55, 113, 129
quota systems 90–92

racism 44–45, 56, 58, 60–61, 73
reading, speed 75
rebellious behavior 3, 51, 126
Renzulli, J. 30, 64
Research Science Institute 141
revitalization xv, 2, 5, 17, 57–72, 123, 134, 135–145
Richardson study 1, 15, 34, 128, 134
Rickover Institute 141
RMC Research Corporation 8
Rogosa, David 141
ROTC 65

Sacramento Association of Gifted Educators 22
Sagan, Carl 129
San Diego 94
SAT 127, 141
Sears, Robert 142
Secondary Education Policy 4
seminar program 17, 34, 44, 47, 50
Shakespeare 46, 47
Shakespeare Festival in Ashland, Oregon 129
Shanker, Albert 142
Short Form Test of Academic Aptitude 27
Shostakovich 101
Silicon Valley 80
Soviet Union 7, 18, 95, 96–102, 122, 127, 142; Basic Principles of the Unified Labour School 96; Education Act 96; intelligence testing 96–97;